12/03

THE SOMME

THE SOMME

GARY SHEFFIELD

CASSELL

Cassell
Wellington House, 125 Strand
London WC2R 0BB

A catalogue record for this book is available
from the British Library.

ISBN 0-304-35704-9

Designed by Goldust Design
Printed and bound in Great Britain by
MPG Books Ltd, Bodmin, Cornwall

940,4272
SHE
2003

CONTENTS

LIST OF MAPS

Map key

56R German Army Units		3 Col. French Army Units	
9 British Army Units		143 Brigade	
3 Col. French Army Units		36 Infantry Division	
		2 Ind. Cavalry Division	
		VIII Corps	
		Fourth Army	

To Jennie, with a father's love

The central panel of Otto Dix's 'War Triptych'. Dix (1891-1969) served as a machine gunner in the German army on the Somme, and his anti-war Expressionist paintings were responses to the horrors of industrialised warfare.

FOREWORD

The battle of the Somme has a unique and unenviable position in British military history. It not only saw the British Army's bloodiest day, 1 July 1916, but was its most costly battle ever, with more British casualties even than Passchendaele the following year. The first day's dreadful poignancy is founded not only on the loss of life, though this was terrible enough, but also on its shocking dislocation of expectation. The men who attacked that day, so many of them in locally-recruited Pals' battalions, believed that this was the 'Big Push' which would end the war: instead, it turned into a bitter attritional struggle which ground on until the autumn. These sombre truths have helped paint the Somme in dark colours, and it stands for some historians, and for many more with a general interest in the war, as a classic example of waste, futility and sheer incompetence. One of the many merits of Gary Sheffield's book is to emphasise that there is another side to the Somme: it was a battle which was strategically essential and, as Paddy Griffith has written, transformed the British Army 'from a largely inexperienced mass army to a largely experienced one.'

First, it was not a battle that the British, coalition partners as they were, could have avoided. The German occupation of a huge swathe of Belgian and French territory in 1914 forged a powerful mainspring for Allied offensives: it was the logic of recovering lost territory and hostage populations, not stubborn folly, that drove the allies to attack time and time again. But if the Somme was already sketched out in principle in late 1915, when Allied leaders decided on an Anglo-French attack astride the Somme the following year, the German assault on Verdun in February 1916 lent new urgency to the offensive, for an attack on the Somme would drag the Germans from the French windpipe at Verdun.

Verdun also changed the Somme's character. Although, as Gary Sheffield very properly observes, French troops fought with distinction on the Somme, making a contribution so often forgotten in anglophone histories, the brunt of the battle was borne by the British.

Second, the Somme played a key role in the development of the British Army. Both World Wars were characterised by its rapid expansion from a pre-war regular force, tiny by the standards of continental war, to huge citizens' armies capable of fighting major operations against a first-rate opponent. The strains inherent in this transition were all too clearly visible in 1916. It was an enthusiastic but patchily-trained British Army that began the Somme. Many of the attackers had not previously been in battle, and there were many officers promoted into posts for which they had neither experience nor proper preparation, simply because there was no alternative. As the battle went on, the British Army ascended a steep and agonising learning-curve, dotted with costly mistakes and missed opportunities, and eventually emerged from the fighting bloodied but improved. Charles Carrington, who saw the battle's roughest edge as an infantry officer, believed that: 'The British Army learnt its lesson the hard way, during the middle part of the Somme battle, and, for the rest of the war, was the best army in the field.'

Gary Sheffield's account not only deals with 1 July in detail (and how right he is to emphasise what historians owe to Martin Middlebrook's ground-breaking work) but goes on to chart the battle's development in the days and weeks that followed. Those sub-sets of the Somme, like Flers-Courcelette, Morval, Thiepval Ridge and the Ancre Heights, their names graven in stone atop the great panes of the Memorial to the Missing at Thiepval, but somehow hard to grasp in isolation, are woven seamlessly together. The air battle, with British air superiority being counterbalanced by a measure of German control after mid-September, as Oswald Boelke and Manfred von Richthofen arrived with new types of aircraft, receives proper attention.

But most of all I admire the way that this measured operational narrative is leavened by the impact of personality. The legendary Australian Lieutenant Albert Jacka should indeed have been awarded a bar to the VC he had earned at Gallipoli; Private 'Todger' Jones of the

Cheshires earned his VC capturing a hundred Germans in the wreckage of Morval; and Lieutenant Colonel Bernard Freyberg's VC, won with the inimitable Royal Naval Division, was regarded by another VC winner as probably the war's most distinguished act of courage. It is this interplay between the individual and the mass that helps remind us of the extraordinary courage and endurance that helped the attackers claw their way across a landscape reduced to wilderness by shellfire, and to point, yet again, to the great truth that even at times when human life counts for little the human spirit reigns supreme: it did so even on the Somme.

Richard Holmes

INTRODUCTION

The Somme is the most notorious battle in British military history. Only Passchendaele runs it close in terms of the malevolence of its popular reputation. The huge losses incurred for meagre territorial gains by the British Army between July and November 1916 mark it out as one of the greatest human tragedies ever to befall these islands. The shock waves of death on an industrial scale spread across the globe, to Canada, Newfoundland, New Zealand, Australia, South Africa, and of course, France and Germany. That single word, 'Somme', the name of a French *département* and river, has come to symbolize all that was wasteful, incompetent and futile about the fighting on the Western Front.

There is another view. This sees the Somme as a necessary, even an inevitable battle that hurt the Germans more than the British and pushed them towards making strategic decisions that would eventually lose them the war. During the course of the battle, an inexperienced British Army underwent a steep learning curve in how to fight a modern war, at a time when conflict was undergoing revolutionary changes. The year 1916 can only be fairly judged if one sees it in the context of the whole war, for the attrition inflicted on the Germans on the Somme and in subsequent battles made possible the victory of 1918. In this view, the Somme was the 'muddy grave' of the Imperial German Army.

I have been fascinated by the Battle of the Somme for most of my life. In my early teens I picked up a second-hand copy of Martin Middlebrook's book *The First Day on the Somme* and was enthralled and appalled in about equal measure. Enthralled, because Middlebrook's brilliant telling of the story of 'Kitchener's Mob', a mass citizen army, captured my imagination. Appalled, because of the terrible casualties suffered by the British Army on 1 July 1916: nearly 60,000 men killed, wounded, missing and taken prisoner, about 20,000 of them fatalities, for apparently so little gain. I wanted to know more, but my local library in south London did not have much on the subject, and I had to content myself with re-reading *The First Day on the Somme* several times. Although dated in some ways, it remains essential reading to this day.

A few years later I read history at the University of Leeds, and took a special subject on 'Britain and the First World War'. My interest in Kitchener's Army and the Somme revived, and ideas I had previously picked up about the 'futility' of the First World War and the incompetence of the British Army began to be challenged.

My initial research interest was into the social history of Kitchener's Army, but the fighting on the Somme was never far behind. As a graduate student in 1984 I made the first of what must now be several score of visits to the Somme battlefields. On that occasion I went on an organized coach party, but in 1986 as a junior lecturer in the Department of War Studies, Royal Military Academy Sandhurst, I spent several days wandering over the battlefields with a friend, seeing areas that were off the beaten tourist track. Then as now there were a series of obvious sites to visit – the Newfoundland Battlefield Park at Beaumont Hamel, the Lochnagar Crater at La Boisselle, Delville Wood – but I found it most rewarding to hunt down the more obscure areas, to get the real 'feel' of the battle. My first visit to a Commonwealth War Graves Commission Cemetery made an impression that is with me still. Serried ranks of headstones, manicured lawns, well-tended flowers – paradoxically, nothing brings the dreadful nature of the fighting home to me more effectively than these idyllic spots, that so well fulfil the original intention of recreating an English country garden overseas.

If *The First Day on the Somme* was one of the foundation stones of my interest in the battle, Robin Prior and Trevor Wilson's *Command on the Western Front*, published in 1992, was the other. Effectively a military biography of General Sir Henry Rawlinson, Fourth Army commander on the Somme, it provided a detailed analysis of the thinking and planning behind the battle. It brought a high level of sophistication to a debate that had too often been conducted along the lines of simply seeing British high command as 'donkeys'. Like that of all historians,

Prior and Wilson's work is not beyond criticism. In particular, they paid little attention to the relationship between Rawlinson and his Chief of Staff, Major General A.A. Montgomery. None the less, *Command on the Western Front* remains a seminal work. Neither Rawlinson nor Haig emerged particularly well from Prior and Wilson's study of the Somme, and my own findings, presented in this book, tend to confirm their analysis, with some modifications.

In this book I have attempted to combine a narrative of the battle with analysis and explanation of why things occurred in the way they did, and some views from the man in the trench. In doing so, I have made use of some primary research, and have synthesized the work of other scholars. The structure of this book is fairly traditional, in that the main focus is on the British Army. However, I have tried not to lose sight of the fact that the British faced the German Army across no man's land, or that the Somme was a coalition battle, in which the French Army played a significant role. I have devoted a disproportionate amount of space to the first day of the battle, although this is justified by the impact of 1 July 1916 on British folk-memory and historiography, as well as its role in shaping the remainder of the campaign. I have also sought to avoid the approach taken by some older accounts of the battle of the Somme, which tended to focus on the peaks (1 July, 14 July, 15 September and the Ancre fighting of 13 November) while paying scant attention to the periods in between. Relatively small-scale actions such as the struggles for Guillemont and Thiepval were in many ways more typical of the fighting on the Somme than the larger and more famous set-piece battles.

Inevitably there is much that I would have preferred to treat at greater length, but this is a short book. I have set the Somme into the wider context of the Great War in my *Forgotten Victory – The First World War: Myths and Realities* (Headline, 2001), and will be examining the tactical and operational issues in more detail in the forthcoming *Haig's Army*, to be co-authored with John Lee and Peter Simkins.

Since the early 1980s, the patient work of scholars basing their work on the archival treasures held in the UK and elsewhere in the Commonwealth have transformed our understanding of Britain in the First World War. Much of the received wisdom established in the 1920s and

1930s by critics of British high command such as Lloyd George and Liddell Hart had been revised or even discredited. The result is a multi-faceted view of the war, which is both more complex and more interesting than the 'bloody fools' school of thought associated with writers such as Alan Clark and John Laffin. Yet much research still remains to be done on the Somme. To pick on just a few areas, our understanding of the intelligence available to Haig, and the use he made of it, is likely to be transformed when Jim Beach's University of London Ph.D. appears. We still know too little about staff work, and the number of excellent studies now available of individual units and formations highlights the diversity of experience on the Somme. Recent writings by William Philpott, Elizabeth Greenhalgh and Brock Millman bear testimony to the vigour of the debates on Anglo-French strategy. We are a very long way from the last word being said about the battle of the Somme.

Many people have contributed to the writing of this book. Professor Richard Holmes asked me to write it for his *Fields of Battle* series, and Keith Lowe, my editor at Cassell, has shown exemplary patience during its protracted gestation. I will be for ever grateful to Dr Hugh Cecil for his kindness and encouragement when he taught me as an undergraduate and then supervised my MA thesis at Leeds University. I owe a great debt to Geoff Inglis for those first battlefield tours, and much else. The archives at the National Portrait Gallery gave me much help at very short notice. I have discussed the Somme over many years with colleagues at Sandhurst, in between periods of forming square to repulse attackers. Dr Stephen Badsey and Mr Lloyd Clark read the book in manuscript and made many valuable suggestions, as did Professor Peter Simkins of the University of Birmingham; any blemishes that remain are of course my responsibility. I have had some stimulating discussions on the First World War with my Staff College colleagues Drs Helen McCartney and Bob Foley, and also Mr John Lee, Professor Brian Bond, Mr Chris McCarthy and Mr Robert Pearson.

It has been rightly said that to write a book one needs to turn over a library – in this case I turned over two, and my profound thanks are due to Mr Andrew Orgill and his staff (Sandhurst), and Mr Chris Hobson and his staff (JSCSC).

Finally, I'd like to thank the members of St John the Baptist's Anglican Church for the welcome they gave the Sheffield family in 2002, and to Viv, Jennie and James, who make it all worth while.

Gary Sheffield
King's College, London, and Joint Services Command and Staff College, Shrivenham
July 2002

ACKNOWLEDGEMENTS

The quotation from the Charles Bonham-Carter papers appears by kind permission of Mr Victor Bonham-Carter. Crown Copyright material appears by kind permission of Her Majesty's Stationery Office. Quotations from the E.W Harris papers appear by kind permission of the University of Leeds. To anyone whose copyright I have unwittingly infringed I offer my sincere apologies.

CHAPTER 1

THE ROAD TO THE SOMME

DIPLOMATIC ORIGINS

In hindsight, there seems to be a sense of terrible inevitability about the battle of the Somme. A series of events occurred which had consequences that led seemingly inexorably to that point on 1 July 1916 when thousands of British soldiers clambered out of their trenches and advanced towards the enemy.

The first was the beginning of the war itself. Wars do not occur by accident, and the conflict that began in August 1914 was no exception to this rule. The behaviour of Germany and Austria–Hungary was the most important factor in bringing about war. Under Otto von Bismarck, the 'Iron Chancellor', Prussia had destroyed the old balance of power in Europe by defeating Austria in 1866 and France in 1870–71, and uniting the various German states into a German Empire under Prussian leadership. This done, Germany settled into and upheld the new balance of power. However Kaiser Wilhelm II, who came to the throne in 1888, chafed at the wise limitations that Bismarck had placed on German ambition. Germany was the most powerful state on the European continent, and after sacking Bismarck, Wilhelm sought *Weltpolitik*, world power, commensurate with this status. His bellicose and clumsy foreign policy had, by July 1914, painted Germany into a corner.

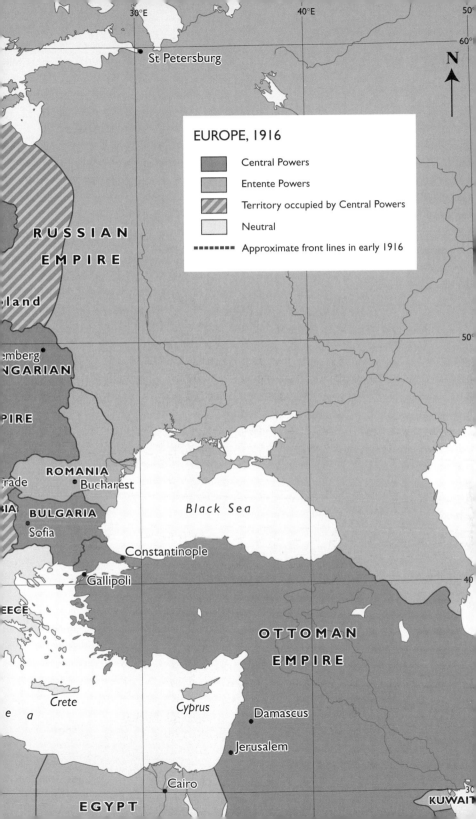

Thoroughly frightened, republican France and tsarist Russia had formed an alliance that on the surface appeared unlikely but reflected shared strategic worries. Britain, which had in the 1890s been mildly pro-German, was jolted out of its position of 'splendid isolation' by an ambitious German programme of naval rearmament that threatened both the *status quo* in Europe and the security of the home islands. Remarkably, by 1914, the British had reached diplomatic accommodation with their two main colonial rivals, France and Russia. This *entente* fell short of a full alliance, but it was clear that Britain had moved into the Franco-Russian camp. In July 1914 Vienna moved against Serbia, following the assassination of the heir apparent to the Austro-Hungarian throne by a Serb nationalist in Sarajevo. There is a strong body of evidence that Germany seized on this excuse to achieve its grand strategic aims, even at the risk of bringing about a general war. Some historians have gone further, arguing that from at least December 1912 onwards the German leadership had been actively planning to go to war in the summer of 1914. Seeking to break out of self-created diplomatic encirclement, and achieve hegemony in Europe, the German leadership risked war in 1914 and embraced it when it occurred. In doing so, Germany took Europe on the first step towards the Somme.

Despite the attempts of some historians to argue to the contrary, Britain had no real alternative to going to war in August 1914. For generations Britain had fought war after war to prevent one state from dominating Europe. As Lord Palmerston famously

Kaiser Wilhelm II of Germany. At the end of the war Wilhelm went into exile. He died in Holland in 1941.

commented in 1848, Britain had 'no eternal allies' or 'perpetual enemies'; rather Britain's 'interests were eternal and perpetual'. Thus since the 1580s wars had been fought, in defence of the balance of power, against Philip II's Spain, the France of Louis XIV, and later Napoleon's French Empire. In 1914 a successful German bid for domination of Europe would have threatened Britain's strategic and economic position. Worse, German possession of Belgium and the French Channel coast would have posed a direct threat to British naval security. These territories were Britain's outer defences, and for centuries Britain had fought to keep them out of the hands of a hostile power. In a very real sense, Britain went to war over Belgium in 1914.

BRITISH STRATEGY 1914–15

Just as in the wars against Louis XIV and Napoleon, in 1914 Britain fought as part of a coalition of states. Britain's immediate contribution was financial and naval. British maritime power was of fundamental importance in winning the First World War. It enabled Britain to keep open the Atlantic lifeline by which supplies and, in 1917–18, American troops crossed from the New World to the Old. The Royal Navy was able to impose a blockade that slowly starved Germany, both literally and metaphorically. There was no decisive naval battle, a second Trafalgar, but simply by remaining unbeaten, the Grand Fleet guaranteed British security; even if the army in France was to be defeated, Germany could not land troops in Britain.

Despite its importance, naval power gave Britain relatively little leverage within the counsels of the Allies. What the French and Russians demanded from Britain was troops on the ground, and lots of them. But Britain's army was small. In August the 100,000-strong British Expeditionary Force (BEF) crossed to the Continent, where it took its place in the line of battle alongside the sixty-two-division French Army. Through a combination of being in the right place at the right time, fighting skill and bloody-minded tenacity, the BEF, initially of four infantry divisions, later of six, played a role out of all proportion to its size in halting the German onslaught.

As the junior partner in the *entente*, to a very large extent Britain had to dance to the French tune. Lord Kitchener, as Secretary of State for War, was responsible for raising the vast citizen volunteer army that came to bear his name. He seems to have intended that this force would make a grand entrance on to the Western Front in about 1917, by which time the continental armies would have been exhausted. Britain could then win the war and dictate the peace to friend and foe alike. His strategy was thrown off course by French demands for Britain to pull its weight now, not at some point in the future. Having lost heavily in the initial stages of the campaign, both France and Russia suffered further horrendous casualties in 1915. After having survived, but only just, the initial German invasion, Paris demanded that British troops take over more miles of line, to free French troops to drive the Germans from their soil. Even better, the British should themselves attack. The Russians, in 1915 the victims of successful German offensives, understandably wanted their allies to relieve the pressure by attacking in the West.

While carrying out some offensives on the Western Front, in 1915 the British also turned to a traditional, and superficially more promising, strategy based on seapower. The 'British Way in Warfare' – the concept of using British naval power to land troops on the peripheries, where they would (in theory) have a disproportionate impact on the war – has a very ancient lineage. In March 1915 an Anglo-French fleet attempted to take the Dardanelles and thus force Germany's ally Turkey out of the war. This was followed by amphibious landings in April on the Gallipoli peninsula. Both attempts ended in failure. A third effort, involving fresh landings at Suvla Bay in August, spelt the end of any realistic hopes of success at Gallipoli. The failure to defeat Turkey is paralleled by a depressingly long list of similar fiascos before and since, the expeditions to Walcheren in 1809 and Norway in 1940 among them. In addition, in August 1915 the Germans inflicted a major defeat on the Russian forces in Poland.

Unanticipated events thus blew Kitchener's strategy off course, and the failure at Gallipoli discredited the attractions of an

'Eastern' strategy, at least temporarily. The result was a fragile strategic consensus that a major effort should be made on the Western Front. Kitchener admitted on 20 August 1915 that 'we had to make war as we must, and not as we should like to.' Twenty-five British divisions were sent to the Western Front in 1915. The battle of Loos, a subsidiary part of a larger French offensive launched in September 1915, saw divisions of Kitchener's Army committed for the first time to a major battle on the Western Front. By the time of his death in May 1916 Kitchener was convinced that Britain needed to make an all-out effort that year.

The events of 1915 saw the triumph of those members of the British elite committed to a total war effort over those who wanted to keep Britain's liability limited. This division blurred the boundaries between proponents of an Eastern strategy, and 'Westerners'. David Lloyd George, the most influential 'Easterner' politician, and General Sir William Robertson, Chief of the Imperial General Staff and the Westerner *par excellence*, were united by the belief that total mobilization of all Britain's resources – human and economic – was a prerequisite for victory. A sign of the dominance of the total warriors was the willingness to become increasingly reliant on US bankers to fund the British war effort, in spite of the long-term economic cost. At the beginning of the war there was a gulf between the demands of British forces for war *matériel*, and the ability of the economy to supply them, leading to shortages of munitions and equipment. By 1916, through mobilization of the economy and the purchase of American *matériel*, the supply was beginning to match the demand. The Germans, too, had created a war economy. The consequence was revealed on the Somme: a *Materielschlacht*, described by a German military commentator as 'a battle of *matériel* which could be fought to a finish only by timely and maximum exertion of all munitions industries'.[1]

DIPLOMATIC AND TACTICAL DEADLOCK

Surveying the carnage of the First World War from a distance of nearly ninety years, an obvious question to pose is why did it not

'YOU ARE THE MAN I WANT'

Lord Kitchener, as depicted on a recruiting poster. Kitchener was the architect of the New Armies that formed the heart of the British forces on the Somme.

end long before 1918 in a compromise peace. The first answer was that the populations of Europe did not want it to. The years 1914 and 1915 were traumatic for the peoples of Europe. Mourning for dead sons, husbands and fathers was compounded by the need to come to terms with a variety of changes to normal life: food shortages, troops billeted on private houses, restrictions on freedom. But the popular enthusiasm shown at the outbreak of war, the 'spirit of 1914', had not completely evaporated. The strain felt on the home fronts of all belligerents in 1917–18 was still some months away.

Moreover, the war aims of the belligerents were irreconcilable. France wished to expel enemy troops from its soil, recover Alsace–Lorraine (annexed by Germany in 1871), and clip Germany's wings. Britain was concerned about the balance of power, and wanted to prise Belgium from Germany's grasp. Both states were near-democracies, although allied to tsarist Russia, and neither relished the idea of the victory of autocratic Germany. Berlin, by contrast, planned to reduce France to a second-class power, to turn Belgium into a protectorate, and to create *Mitteleuropa*, a German-dominated economic zone in the centre of Europe. By the end of the war, Germany was busy carving an empire out of the ruins of defeated Russia. These expansionist plans had a good deal of continuity with those of the Third Reich. They lacked the racist and consciously genocidal elements central to Nazi methods, although Imperial Germany's policies in occupied territories were harsh enough. Despite some desultory diplomatic moves by the belligerents, in 1916 there was not enough common ground for a compromise peace to be reached, and little popular demand for one in any case. The fight would go on.

This diplomatic deadlock was complemented by a tactical stalemate. The fundamental reason why a decision was not reached on the battlefield was that the armies had reached a tactical impasse on the Western Front. The defensive had a temporary advantage, as the armies dug in and created increasingly formidable trench systems covered by belts of barbed wire. All armies were armed with broadly similar weapons: quick-firing artillery, which in the case of the British 18-pounder, the standard field gun, fired out to 6,524 yards; a bolt-action rifle with an effective range of about 600 yards; and a machine-gun with a range of 2,000 yards and a rate of fire of between 450 and 600 rounds per minute. As the war progressed, other weapons were introduced, including some designed for conditions of static warfare: trench mortars, flame-throwers, hand-grenades and tanks. Not until the last months of the war did one side – the Allies, and specifically the British – achieve a margin of technological superiority so great as to be decisive. In July 1916 tactics and techniques were still fairly rudimentary, particularly in the British Army.

On the battlefield, commanders were greatly hampered by the problem of communications. The First World War was fought in a technological hiatus; armies were too big and too dispersed for commanders to exercise voice control in person, yet radio communications were in the most rudimentary of states. Once the infantry went over the top, commanders could have little influence over what happened next. Even if a breakthrough was achieved and a message reached higher command to this effect, the lack of a usable instrument of exploitation (i.e. troops that could move faster than the retreating infantry) meant that pursuit was immensely difficult. Horsed cavalry were mostly obsolete on the Western Front, although on occasion they could be effective – one of these moments was to occur on the Somme on 14 July 1916. Tanks were only introduced in September 1916, and were slow, unreliable and incapable of maintaining a sustained pursuit. These realities were imperfectly understood in July 1916.

ALLIED STRATEGY FOR 1916

At the end of 1915 the BEF gained a new Commander-in-Chief (C-in-C). General Sir Douglas Haig was a 55-year-old Lowland Scot. A cavalryman by background, he had made his name in the Sudan campaign in 1898 and then in the Second Boer War. He was socially well connected, having the ear of the king. There was more to Haig than social ambition, however. The poor performance of

Left to right, Albert Thomas, (French Socialist cabinet minister) General Sir Douglas Haig; General Joffre; David Lloyd George. As this picture suggests, the Haig/Lloyd George relationship was a difficult one.

the British Army in the Boer War had led to a series of important reforms. Haig had played a significant part in this process, working closely with Richard Burdon Haldane, the Secretary of State for War in Asquith's Liberal government. Haldane was one of the most distinguished statesmen ever to hold this position, and the fact that he thought highly of Haig speaks volumes. When war broke out in August 1914 Haig commanded I Corps at Aldershot. This was an important appointment. Haig took I Corps to France, and he later recalled the understandable 'pride with which I took the field along with them'.[2] Haig was promoted to command First Army on its formation at the end of the year. Haig's chance came after the battle of Loos in September 1915, which was mishandled by the C-in-C, Field Marshal Sir John French. Haig undoubtedly intrigued against his C-in-C, but few doubted that French should go or that Haig was the man to succeed him. The Somme was to be his first major battle as C-in-C, so to some extent Haig was on trial; however, there was no obvious pretender to his crown.

On Haig's appointment as C-in-C, his political superior, Kitchener, issued him with a set of instructions. These stressed that Haig's 'governing policy' should be to 'achieve... the closest co-operation of French and British as a united army'. However, Kitchener continued: 'I wish you distinctly to understand that your command is an independent one, and that you will in no case come under the orders of any Allied General further than the necessary co-operation with our Allies above referred to.'[3] Successive commanders of the BEF had the worst of all worlds: having to juggle the maintenance of independence with falling in with French wishes, without enjoying the compensations of true unity of command. In September 1915 Sir John French had, against his better judgement, fought the battle of Loos over the broken terrain of pit villages and winding gear at the behest of French high command. At the dawn of 1916, it was clear that the British Army was going to have to fight a major action somewhere during the course of the year, if only to maintain the solidity of the alliance.

Allied strategy for 1916 was thrashed out at a meeting of Allied leaders at Chantilly in December 1915. The strategy was to take the form of offensives launched by Russia, Italy and Franco-British forces. The idea of the major Allies acting in concert to attack the Germans on three fronts was perfectly sensible, and Haig, who inherited the responsibility of executing the British portion of the plan, fully recognized the importance of tying down German forces on the BEF's front, to prevent them redeploying elsewhere. This did not mean that he necessarily wanted to fight on the Somme. At the beginning of 1916 the British began planning for an offensive in the Ypres area. At a meeting on 20 January, Joffre agreed to the major British effort taking place in Flanders in the summer, with the BEF launching a subsidiary battle on the Somme in the spring. This was in accordance with Joffre's preference for a two-stage campaign, the first operation to wear out the enemy and force the Germans to commit their reserves, and the second to deliver the *coup de grâce*. This concept fell foul of British uneasiness about casualties, the inability of Russia to attack before the summer, and the unwillingness of the Belgians to co-operate in an offensive in Flanders. On 14 February Haig and Joffre agreed to attack on the Somme at the beginning of July. Seven days later, however, Falkenhayn launched a major attack at Verdun.

THE CONSEQUENCES OF VERDUN

When the war began, General Erich von Falkenhayn (1861–1922) was the German Minister of War. The failure of the Schlieffen Plan propelled him in September 1914 to the position of Chief of the General Staff – *de facto* Commander-in-Chief of the German Army. Since then he had had a good track record. German armies had stabilized the situation in the West; they had not won the war, but they had not lost it either. In 1915 German forces had overrun Serbia and pushed the Russians out of much of Poland. Falkenhayn was virtually unique among senior commanders of all the belligerent nations in being willing to contemplate something less than total victory, which suggests that he had a very firm grasp on the strategic realities that faced the Germans: they faced a coalition with superior resources. In November 1914 he presented what

*Erich von Falkenhayn. German failures at Verdun and the Somme
led to his dismissal as de facto commander-in-chief.*

has been described as an 'astonishingly realistic' evaluation of the
Central Powers' strategic position, advising a diplomatic line of
operations to split the enemy coalition by making concessions.[4]

Historians still dispute exactly what Falkenhayn sought to
achieve at Verdun. In his post-war memoirs he claimed to have
presented a memorandum to the kaiser at Christmas 1915 arguing
for an attritional offensive to bleed the French Army white, and
thus force the French into a compromise peace, albeit favourable
to Germany. Various decisions support this view, particularly the
German failure to attempt to cut the *Voie Sacrée*, the 'sacred road'
from Verdun to Bar-le-Duc that represented the French Army's

only communication route to the battlefield. Against this interpretation is the problem that the Christmas memorandum has not survived, and the suspicion remains that Falkenhayn was trying to explain away the failure to break through.[5] None the less, Falkenhayn's interpretation does fit the facts quite well, and is certainly in keeping with his overall strategic vision. Be that as it may, the battle rapidly escalated; Crown Prince Wilhelm, the commander of Fifth Army, apparently did not believe that the battle should be kept limited, and may not have been privy to Falkenhayn's strategy.

Verdun caused profound changes to the concept of the Somme offensive. The French rose to the bait and decided to defend what had become a symbol of French resistance. Increasing numbers of French troops were committed to fight. As a consequence extreme pressure was placed on the British to launch a premature offensive to take the strain off their hard-pressed ally at Verdun. Falkenhayn seems to have hoped that the BEF would do just this, and that having defeated the BEF's attack the Germans would then go on to the counter-offensive. Haig would have preferred to fight as late as possible in 1916, to allow his troops time to train and prepare, and for sufficient supplies of artillery – particularly heavy guns – and ammunition to reach the BEF. Just three months before the Somme offensive commenced, Haig confided in his diary that 'I have not got an army in France really, but a collection of divisions untrained for the field. The actual fighting Army will be evolved from them.'[6]

Moreover, Haig would rather have fought at Ypres, where there were some real strategic objectives, not least the Belgian coast.[7] The British were hypersensitive about the threat that enemy occupation of this area posed to British security, and such fears were not without foundation, as the 1917 campaign of unrestricted submarine warfare was to demonstrate. However, strategic realities – the dominating role of the French within the alliance, and specifically the appalling pressures being placed on the French Army at Verdun – meant that the British had to fall in line, as far as

Next page: The ruins of Rue St Pierre, Verdun. The struggle at Verdun forced the BEF to take on the main burden of the fighting on Allied offensive on the Somme.

possible, with French demands.

Anglophone historians have often treated the Somme as a purely British battle. Yet that is to forget that the French Army had a substantial role, and the French C-in-C, General Joseph Joffre, was an important figure in the offensive. 'Papa' Joffre (1852–1931) had done much, through his calm generalship, to save France during the German invasion in 1914. In 1915 his attempts to expel German forces from French soil through a series of large-scale attacks had resulted in huge casualty lists but little tangible gain. Joffre was not a formal coalition Commander-in-Chief. 'My role in co-ordinating the action of the Allied forces,' Joffre later wrote, was possible 'thanks solely to the consent of the Commanders-in-Chief of the Coalition... no agreement of any kind conferred upon me authority over the Allied armies'.[8] In effect, the naturally autocratic Joffre acted as the director of the Franco-British offensive on the Somme; he could not give Haig orders, but none the less his wishes could not be ignored.

What did Haig think the BEF was going to achieve? From his days as a student at the Staff College, Camberley, Haig had learned that battles were conducted in three stages: a preliminary, attritional, 'wearing-out' fight, that would draw in the enemy reserves; then would come the decisive blow, which would lead to the exploitation phase, the pursuit of a beaten enemy. In January 1916 Haig had rejected the idea of a purely attritional battle in favour of an offensive intended to be decisive.[9] However, over the next months Haig began to envisage the Somme as an attritional battle. Haig had become alarmed at the impact that Verdun was having on his ally; the 'mill on the Meuse' seemed to be grinding away at the French Army's fighting power, its morale and ability to take the offensive. Haig, who was to have been a supporting actor in a predominantly French battle with British support, instead took the leading role. As William Philpott has argued, both Joffre and Haig became less optimistic as to the likely result of the battle. For Joffre, the idea that the Somme would be the decisive act of the war was replaced by a hope that it would take pressure off Verdun, and perhaps ease the path of the Russians by tying down German divisions in France. Similarly, by May 1916 Haig's assessment of what the Somme would achieve was significantly more modest than he was suggesting at the turn of the year; it had become the wearing-out battle that he and Joffre had agreed upon. Indeed, the idea of an offensive in Flanders was revived, should the French Army be so debilitated by Verdun that it was unable to join in an attack on the Somme. As Philpott concludes: 'For Britain the Somme was a battle fought for intangible strategic gains, to sustain an ally as much as defeat the enemy.'[10]

Haig was only six months into a job for which little in his previous experience had prepared him, and he was still coming to terms with the realities of high command. He had not discounted the possibility of a breakthrough, as his ambitious operational plans (see below) make clear. He seems to have wanted to cover all options: to dampen down expectations (as Haig's intelligence chief commented in his diary on 30 June: 'it is always well to disclaim great hopes before an attack'[11]) if the battle did turn out be an attritional affair; but also to achieve a decisive victory, if that proved possible. This was another example of the ambiguities inherent in the British concept for the Somme.

THE TERRAIN

The battle of the Somme was to be fought over terrain that reminded many soldiers of southern England; rolling downs, fields and woods. For men who had moved from the Ypres Salient, the change of scenery from the 'dreary, drab and depressing surroundings of Flanders to the open plains of the Somme' lifted their spirits.[12] Just behind the British front line was Albert, a small town dominated by a large basilica. Early in the war, a shell had hit the basilica and dislodged a large gilded statue of the Virgin holding the infant Christ. The statue leaned out at a precarious angle over the street, giving rise to the idea that Mary was offering Jesus as propitiation for man's sins; a more prosaic legend was that the war would only end once the statue had fallen.

The key to the battlefield was the chalk ridge that sprawled from

Thiepval in the west to Morval in the east, with the village of Pozières lying on the highest point of the ridge. A long, arrow-straight Roman road ran across the right centre of the ridge, connecting Albert with Bapaume, the latter behind the German front line. The German First Position was situated on the forward slope of the ridge, incorporating the villages of Serre, Beaumont Hamel, Thiepval, Ovillers, La Boisselle, Fricourt and Mametz. Even before the defenders carried out improvements to their position, this would have been a tough nut to crack. The ridge petered out in spurs of land and small valleys, where carefully situated machine-guns created interlocking fields of fire. South of the Albert–Bapaume road, the ground was a less formidable obstacle for the assaulting troops, and this was to be reflected in the ground gained on the first day of the offensive. A small river, the Ancre, wound its way in the northern part of the battlefield, its banks bordered by marshy areas. A much bigger river, the Somme, lay in the French sector.

The term 'front line' is rather misleading, as it consisted of at least three trenches separated by 150 to 200 yards. Dug-outs were positioned up to 30 feet beneath the ground, providing protection for twenty-five men. Behind the First Position was an intermediate series of strongpoints, such as the Schwaben Redoubt near Thiepval; and the Second Position ran from Grandcourt to Longueval, via Mouquet Farm and the rear of Pozières. In the area of the Second Position were villages such as the Bazentins, Guillemont and Maurepas, and wooded areas: Delville and High Woods in particular were to gain notoriety. Yet a Third Position lay behind this area, running from Achiet le Petit in the north to the rear of Combles. Begun in February 1916, it was still under construction when the battle began.

For all the formidable nature of the defensive position, it contained two serious flaws. Situated as it was on a forward slope, the First Position was exposed to Allied artillery fire, a problem compounded by the crowding of troops into front-line trenches. Falkenhayn insisted that ground lost to an enemy attack should be recaptured without delay. This encouraged the situation where, at the beginning of the Somme battle, 'the normal disposition of a front-line regiment was to have two battalions in or near the front trench system and its third battalion partly near the strongpoints in the intermediate line and partly in the Second Line, that is all within 2,000 yards of the front line and the bulk within 1,000 yards of it.'[13]

Undoubtedly, this tendency to put troops 'on display' magnified German casualties from Allied artillery.

THE PLANS

Haig's concept of operations for the first day of the battle was highly ambitious. First the artillery was to crush German resistance, and then infantry was to advance and punch a hole in the defenders' lines. Haig envisaged Fourth Army capturing the German forward defences on a front of 27,000 yards, from Serre to the junction with the French Army in the area of Montauban. Simultaneously, Third Army would carry out a diversionary operation on Fourth Army's left flank around Gommecourt. In the next phase, Fourth Army was to take the German Second Position on the high ground that stretched from the River Ancre in the north to Pozières, followed by a blow against the Second Position south of the Albert–Bapaume road. This would put Fourth Army in place to attack the weak German Third Position, again south of the Bapaume road, in the Flers area, and then Reserve Army, which included three cavalry divisions, could begin the exploitation phase, striking east and then north towards Arras.[14]

The main burden of the British effort on the Somme was thus to be borne by Fourth Army, commanded by General Sir Henry Rawlinson. Three years younger than Haig, 'Rawly' was an infantryman, with a background in the socially elite 60th Rifles and Coldstream Guards. In common with most of his peers, Rawlinson had learned his trade in colonial small wars in India and Burma, and, like Haig, the Sudan and South Africa. After divisional command at the beginning of the war, he commanded IV Corps in 1915, and formed Fourth Army in February 1916. The

Somme was to be his first major battle as an Army commander. He enjoyed Haig's trust, and his experiences before the Somme led to him to advocate a policy of limited attacks. After the battle of Neuve Chapelle in March 1915, he wrote:

> The enemy are not yet sufficiently demoralized to hunt them with cavalry ... What we want to do now is what I call, 'bite and hold'. Bite off a piece of the enemy's line... and hold it against counter attack. The bite can be made without much loss, and, if we choose the right place and make every preparation to put it quickly into a state of defence, there ought to be no difficulty in holding it against the enemy's counter-attacks, and in inflicting on him at least twice the loss that we have suffered in making the bite.[15]

Rawlinson's idea of how to fight the Somme was broadly similar, and thus differed markedly from Haig's. The Fourth Army commander recognized the strength of the German defences, and in April put forward his scheme of attack. It resembled Haig's in that both saw that weight of artillery fire would be vital, but while the C-in-C saw this as the preliminary to a breakthrough, Rawlinson believed that capture of the Somme ridges should be an end in itself. The Germans, if they were not to cede possession of key terrain that allowed the British to dominate their defences, would be forced to counter-attack. Rawlinson proposed to smash up the German attacks, and then repeat the process. Haig did not approve of this plan, and Rawlinson was forced to think again. That the C-in-C and the operational commander had very different concepts, and that the latter lacked faith in the plan that was eventually imposed on him did not bode well for the future. Indeed, one might legitimately enquire whether, in the circum-stances, Rawlinson should have been entrusted with the attack. However, Haig continued to have confidence in him. In any case, to put a new commander in place at a late stage would have been politically difficult and have created a number of practical problems.

The commander of Third Army, General Sir Edmund Allenby, played little more than a walk-on part on the Somme. Allenby, also a cavalryman, was a contemporary and rival of Haig's. A third cav-

THE SOMME, 1916:
TOPOGRAPHY & HAIG'S PLAN

——— German Front Line, 1st July

Planned attacks by the
British/French armies

Land over 160m
130 – 160m
100 – 130m
70 – 100m
40 – 70m
Land under 40m

N

0   1   2   3   4   5

Miles

alry officer, General Sir Hubert Gough, commanded Reserve Army. Gough was Haig's protégé, and his force was originally intended to exploit the success to be achieved by Fourth Army at the beginning of the offensive. In the event, Reserve Army was to become the junior partner in the battleline beside Fourth Army. Gough was just 46, and had enjoyed a remarkable rise

in the British Army's pecking order, from commanding a brigade in August 1914 to commanding an army less than two years later. For both Gough and Allenby, the Somme would be the first battle in which they commanded at Army level.

One factor thus united Haig and his Army commanders: that they had no previous experience of command at the level that they were called upon to perform on the Somme. Haig had to step up to command what amounted to an Army Group of some sixty divisions; at Loos his First Army had contained fifteen. Two of Haig's corps commanders at that time had been Rawlinson (IV Corps of three divisions) and Gough (I Corps, four divisions). The pattern was often repeated at lower levels. This was the price that Britain paid for a massive expansion of its army: men were put into positions of responsibility of which they had no experience. Neither had they any training. At the Staff College in Camberley before the war, no thought was given to the handling of anything larger than the six-division Expeditionary Force. This was a stark contrast with their counterparts in the French and German armies, who had trained and thought about conducting large-scale

Above: General Sir Hubert Gough, commander of Reserve Army on the Somme. A protégé of Haig's, Gough remains one of the most controversial generals of the Great War.

Left: General Sir Henry Rawlinson, commander of Fourth Army. Rawlinson's performance on the Somme was patchy, but his finest hour was to come during the final offensives of the war in 1918.

warfare. The colonial-warfare background of senior British commanders had many virtues, not least flexibility in dealing with unexpected situations. British commanders such as Haig were to needed every ounce of this flexibility in dealing with the vast forces that almost no one had anticipated before the war. While many rose to the occasion, some did not.

Aside from Joffre, three other French generals were to play a major role on the Somme. One, Alfred Micheler (1861–1931), the commander of Tenth Army, fought on the extreme right of the Allied battlefront from September onwards. His army was rapidly reduced, as he put it, 'to the role of watchdog for Fayolle' and as such Micheler had relatively little interaction with the British.[16] By contrast, Ferdinand Foch (1851–1929), commander of the French Northern Army Group from 3 July 1916 onwards, became responsible for co-ordinating the French effort with the British on the Somme. His relations with the British were reasonably good. Two years later, Foch and Haig were to enjoy a spiky but productive relationship after the former was appointed as Allied Generalissimo. The commander of French Sixth Army, operating on Rawlinson's immediate right, was General Marie Emile Fayolle (1852–1928). Fayolle was a beneficiary of Joffre's ruthless cull of commanders deemed to have failed in the first two years of the war. A gunner by background, Fayolle was called out of retirement in 1914 to lead an infantry division. A mere eighteen months later, in February 1916, he was appointed to command an army.

Rawlinson's relations with both Foch and Fayolle were generally good. The men had a series of bilateral and trilateral meetings before the battle, and disputes were resolved by compromise. Co-operation during the battle itself proved a greater test of the three men's goodwill, but their relationship survived, intact if a little the worse for wear.

THE GERMAN RESPONSE

By March 1916 Falkenhayn was becoming dissatisfied with the Verdun offensive, which was proving costly to the Germans as well as the French. In February–March he had considered five schemes for attacks on other sectors, including at Ypres, on the Chemin des Dames, and at Arras. He had rejected them all because of the resources that he would have needed to commit, and also the time needed to prepare the attack. Despite his misgivings, for the battle was not unfolding to his satisfaction, Falkenhayn decided to persevere with Verdun. The first signs of British preparations for the Somme offensive became apparent, largely through aerial reconnaissance, to the Germans on 7 April, but at first they were not taken too seriously.[17] The Germans had a low opinion of the fighting capabilities of the British New Armies; they were assessed as having 'high morale' but 'limited combat value'. It is likely that Falkenhayn was planning a major counter-offensive against the British, using Crown Prince Rupprecht of Bavaria's Sixth Army north of the Somme sector, once the Allied attack had been repulsed. This he hoped would be decisive. [18]

However, by 2 June Allied preparations in the Somme area were regarded as sufficiently threatening by General Fritz von Below (1853–1918), commander of Second Army covering the Somme area, for him to request extra forces to make a spoiling attack in the Ancre area. Only two days later the Russian summer offensive, named after its leading figure, General Brusilov, achieved surprise against the Austro-Hungarian army and began a severe crisis for the Central Powers. Falkenhayn had to deploy German forces to the Eastern Front to prop up his ally, and the idea of a German preventative offensive on the Somme was forgotten. Second Army was to pay the price, bearing the brunt of the offensive, for which, however, von Below had some time to prepare. As it was, Falkenhayn redeployed only four divisions plus heavy artillery to meet the forthcoming Allied offensive on the Somme. On 1 July von Below had six divisions in the front line (121st, 12th, 28th Reserve, 26th Reserve, 52nd and 2nd Guard Reserve) with an additional four and a half in reserve. Falkenhayn was gambling on the French being too weakened by Verdun to play much of a role, and by the British being as ineffective as German intelligence predicted. It was a gamble that came perilously close to failing.

THE ARMIES

The German Army on the Somme in July 1916 had endured two years of war. In 1915 Germany had suffered 169,000 dead on the Western Front, and the fighting at Verdun was to add another 80–100,000. In spite of this, the army still contained a fair proportion of soldiers with pre-war experience; the Germans had a form of peace-time conscription, which gave them a large pool of men with some form of military experience on which to draw. The Germans often kept their troops in one sector for months at a time, and so many of those in place at the beginning of the Somme had escaped service at Verdun. The field forces had changed considerably since the heady days of 1914. They looked different. The *pickelhaube* spiked helmet was in the process of disappearing from the battlefield, to be replaced by the 'coal scuttle' *Stahlhelm* (steel helmet) that came to characterize the German soldier in the two world wars. This seemed to symbolize the adaptation of the German Army to the murderous and unglamorous reality of industrialized warfare. It had learned tactical lessons from the earlier battles, and applied them; specialist units of storm-troopers were beginning to be introduced, for example. On the Somme, German troops were to prove tenacious in defence and relentless in counter-attack.

France too had maintained a conscript army in peace-time, and it too had lost heavily in the opening years of the war: 955,000 casualties by the end of 1914, a staggering 1.43 million by the end of 1915. With a smaller population than Germany, France was forced to dig deep into its reserves of manpower. Unlike the British or Germans, France drew extensively on its non-white colonial population to provide troops for the Western Front; Senegalese and North Africans in particular served in large numbers in front-line units. The appalling losses suffered by the pre-war officer corps at the beginning of the war led to mass commissioning from the ranks. This dilution of the quality of the officers perhaps had an adverse effect on the performance of the French Army later in the war. The French had also adapted their fighting methods to the

An obviously posed photograph of German troops en route to the Somme. The scale and violence of the Allied offensive forced Falkenhayn to rush reinforcements to the Somme front.

new conditions of fighting. The change from the *képis*, dark blue jackets and red trousers of 1914 to the 'horizon blue' uniforms and 'Adrian' steel helmets of the Somme period, like the German adoption of the *Stahlhelm*, symbolized the adaptation to modern total war. In 1916 the French Army's resilience proved remarkable. Not only did it endure Verdun, but it confounded Falkenhayn's expectations by playing a significant role in the Somme offensive.

The British Army was very different from those of its major ally and enemy. Alone of the major powers in Europe, Britain's army had been a long-service professional force in 1914; the political market would not bear conscription, despite considerable agitation for it. The small regular army had been largely destroyed by the end of 1914. In the autumn, Lord Kitchener had presciently begun to raise a large army of volunteers, which initiated one of the greatest mass movements in British history. The resulting New (or Kitchener's) Armies contained a number of units raised

The 1/14th Londons (London Scottish). This Territorial Force battalion fought at Gommecourt on the first day of the Somme offensive.

through civic pride. The eight 'Pals' battalions of Tyneside Scottish and Tyneside Irish raised in the north-east of England were examples. Other men joined units that reflected their background or interests, such as the 1st and 2nd Sportsmen's Battalions (23rd and 24th Royal Fusiliers) or Public Schools Battalion (16th Middlesex). In addition, the government raised a substantial number of New Army units. All were added as extra battalions to existing regiments. The voluntary impulse was replicated in the white dominions. Troops from Australia, Canada, New Zealand and South Africa fought on the Somme, as did soldiers from other parts of the empire, including India and Newfoundland.

For both civilians in khaki and the regular army with which they came into contact, the process of adjusting to army life could be difficult. Lecturing to American officers in 1918, a British lieutenant colonel, drawing on his experience, stated that in an army composed of civilians in uniform, with 'an almost total absence of regular army officers' and NCOs, 'the problem of how to maintain discipline is a vexed one'.[19] For all that, the British Army during the war proved to be highly disciplined and effective. The creation of a mass army and an economy capable of sustaining a total war against Imperial Germany was one of the greatest achievements of the British state and people in the twentieth century.

By the end of 1915 units of the New Armies were reaching France to join the regulars and territorials, the latter being part-time soldiers whose units had done much to hold the line in 1915 before the arrival of the Kitchener divisions. The Territorial Force (TF) had also expanded greatly in 1914–15, but this fact has tended to be unfairly overshadowed by the raising of Kitchener's Armies. Although conscription was introduced in January 1916, it was only towards the end of the battle of the Somme that soldiers who had not volunteered began to join the ranks of the fighting units.

The BEF of July 1916 was thus composed of partly surviving pre-war regular and territorial soldiers but mainly of wartime volunteers, many of whom filled the ranks of regular or territorial units already on the Western Front. Although many citizen soldiers had seen active service in 1915, the Somme was to be the first major test of something then unique in British history: a citizen army large enough to play a role in continental-scale warfare. The army that attacked on 1 July 1916 was thus essentially a force of volunteer citizen soldiers.

PREPARATIONS FOR ATTACK: AIR

By 1916 battles were fought in three dimensions, and this was the year that airpower came of age. Before the war, military aviation had largely been seen as the preserve of a few specialists. Some senior commanders had been dismissive of the military potential of the aeroplane. The emergence of trench warfare opened the eyes of most of the doubters. Aeroplanes could fulfil the role that was now denied to the traditional instrument of reconnaissance, cavalry. More than that, as it became clear that the battlefield was dominated by artillery, aircraft proved highly useful in spotting for the gunners: indicating the fall of shot, and thus improving the accuracy of artillery fire.

During 1915 various techniques associated with this new role were developed, key among them photographing the enemy trenches and interpreting the resulting images, and establishing wireless communications between air and ground. So valuable was aerial reconnaissance that aircraft, mostly unarmed at the outbreak of war, spawned a type that would later be termed fighters, which sought to prevent enemy observation aeroplanes from crossing friendly lines, or to protect friendly machines in their role of observation. Thus a battle for control of the air began to develop. The fighting at Verdun in February 1916 was the first major battle in which a struggle for air supremacy played an integral part.

In the course of 1915 Haig, whatever his initial reservations, became an extremely 'air-minded' commander. He enjoyed a good relationship with Major General Hugh Trenchard, the commander of the Royal Flying Corps (RFC), and saw the importance of achieving air superiority during the build-up to the Somme offensive. Haig, typically, having found a subordinate he trusted, largely gave Trenchard a free hand. Like Haig, 'Boom' Trenchard was

A BE2C aeroplane of the Royal Flying Corps. The battles of Verdun and the Somme represented milestones in the evolution of tactical airpower.

committed to an aggressive strategy. In 'Future Policy in the Air', a document issued in September 1916, Trenchard defended his approach of maintaining a constant and unrelenting offensive, aiming to pin German aircraft to their side of no man's land and win psychological and moral dominance over German ground forces.[20] This policy of dominating the skies had a price. Constant offensive patrols took a toll of both aircrew's nerves and aircraft. Between 1 July and the end of the battle of the Ancre, the RFC lost 782 aircraft and 576 pilots from all causes.[21] The German air service had a general policy of remaining on the defensive.

For the battle of the Somme Trenchard had more aircraft than ever before at his disposal. At the time of Loos in September 1915, the RFC had twelve squadrons, but this total had expanded to twenty-seven by July 1916. The squadrons, of eighteen aircraft, were composed of various types: the obsolescent BE2 C; the newer RFC maid of all work, the FE2 B; the DH2 scout; the French

Nieuport 16 scout (the type flown by the British 'ace' Captain Albert Ball VC) and the Sopwith $1^1/2$ Strutter, the first British aircraft with an interrupter gear that allowed a machine-gun to fire through the propeller arc, which gave it considerable potential as a fighter aircraft. They were opposed by the Fokker E III, an improved version of the aeroplane that had dominated the skies from September 1915 onwards, leading to the RFC pilots dubbing themselves 'Fokker fodder'.

The air war on the Western Front saw frequent swings of the pendulum. In July and August 1916 it very definitely moved in the favour of the Allies. As we will see, with some justice many of the German defenders blamed the weight and effectiveness of British and French shelling on the apparently ever-present Allied captive observation balloons and aircraft. Conversely, when poor weather or other factors limited the opportunities of the RFC to observe, this had an adverse impact on the accuracy of artillery fire and thus on the chances of a ground attack succeeding.

LOGISTICS

Today the word 'logistics' is used to refer to the movement and supply of military forces, although the British Army of 1916 used the term 'administration'. The preparations for the Somme involved the greatest logistic challenge the BEF had yet to face. The bayonet strength of the BEF grew from 450,000 to 660,000 in the first half of 1916. The plan for the Somme required 400,000 men and 100,000 horses (the vast majority of the latter used for essential transportation tasks) to be moved, billeted, fed and watered. Shells, ammunition and hand-grenades had to be stockpiled; vehicles kept supplied with fuel and spare parts; trenches improved, and jumping-off points constructed. Seven thousand miles of signal cable was buried beneath the ground. Even so, this list of logistic and engineering preparations barely scratches the surface.[22] The corollary was that logistic troops worked strenuously as the attack approached. 'Very busy day doing repair work for Trench Mortar battery,' noted an Army Service Corps officer in his diary on the eve of the attack. 'Went to Albert 3 times. Terrific shelling going on all the time...' [23] As in all modern warfare, the Somme offensive was founded on a vast logistic infrastructure.

As the campaign developed, further logistic challenges unfolded. To take one of many examples, a conference was held at Advanced GHQ on 15 July to work out how the volume of road and rail traffic would be managed in case of a major advance.[24] Throughout the offensive, the BEF used over 1 million shells every week. As recent research has demonstrated, the prodigious effort on the Somme placed the BEF's logistics under severe strain. Indeed, even if Haig had achieved his much desired breakthrough followed by the revival of mobile warfare, it could not have been supported logistically. It would take more experience and an important reorganization of the BEF's transport by a civilian expert, Sir Eric Geddes, before this would become possible.[25]

IMMEDIATE PRE-BATTLE PREPARATIONS

The final attack plan committed to battle four British corps, a total of thirteen infantry divisions: seven New Army (plus another brigade), two territorial, four nominally regular. French Sixth Army attacked with six divisions. The British preliminary bombardment was intended to last for six days, but wet weather on 26 and 27 June led GHQ to decide to postpone the attack for twenty-four hours, so the bombardment was extended to a full week. Fourth Army deployed 1,010 field guns and howitzers, 182 heavy guns, 245 heavy howitzers. In addition there were forty French howitzers and guns, and sixty French 75mm guns for firing gas shell. This was a substantial increase on the numbers of weapons available in previous years. The British artillery were set three main tasks: cutting the barbed wire in front of the German positions with shrapnel; the destruction of German trenches; and counter-battery work, that is destroying or at least neutralizing the German artillery.

The watching infantry were impressed by the power of the bombardment. An officer of 56th Division described this period as:

A dump of trench mortar ammunition at Acheux, 28 June 1916. Preparations for a First World War offensive posed formidable challenges to logisticians.

days of terror for the enemy. Slowly our guns broke forth upon them in a tumult of rage... [The Germans'] feeble retaliation was swallowed up and overpowered by the torrent of metal that now poured incessantly into their territory... Guns of all calibres pounded their system of trenches till it looked for all the world like nothing more than a ploughed field.[26]

On much of the front, however, the bombardment was visually impressive but was ultimately unsuccessful. Banks of barbed wire remained uncut; German trenches, although battered, still contained determined groups of defenders; and sufficient German artillery survived the counter-battery work to inflict dreadful casualties on the attackers. Rawlinson's original 'bite and hold' concept for the battle was to mount fairly limited attacks, to a depth of 1,250 yards, capture the front line and few objectives beyond it. This shallow advance was sensible, in that it could be supported by artillery, but the 20,000-yard attack frontage was too

wide for the number of guns available. The problem was exacerbated by Haig's insistence on the capture of a greater depth of trench, an average of 2,500 yards. This ensured that artillery support was spread fatally thin. Instead of concentrating firepower, it was dispersed. Too few guns were given too much to do.[27] This was unknown to the assault infantry, who by 7.00 a.m. on 1 July 1916 were sheltering in front-line positions, waiting for the signal to advance. Morale was high. One can easily exaggerate the extent to which the attackers were inexperienced 'lambs led to the slaughter', but there is little doubt that there was a tremendously high level of expectation among the waiting men. Some may have believed that it would be a walk-over, that the artillery would kill or disable all the defenders, but most anticipated having to fight before achieving success. This was to be the major baptism of fire for Kitchener's Army, and failure was unthinkable. At 7.20 a.m., with ten minutes to go, the bombardment intensified, and a huge explosion rocked the northern sector as the mine under Hawthorn Redoubt was detonated. Eight minutes later, the other mines went up. Two minutes to go until zero hour.

The men were ready, bayonets fixed, rifles loaded, the heavy uncomfortable packs finally adjusted. Young officers, many at school a year ago, stood with whistles in their mouths, looking at their watches as the last few seconds ticked away.

The battle was in the hands of these men, now; the generals could do nothing. For the first half hour it would not even be a battalion commander's battle. The outcome would be decided by captains and second-lieutenants, lance corporals and privates. Hearts thud, stomachs turn. 'For God's sake, let us get going.'[28]

At 7.30 a.m. there was a brief period of silence, as the British gunners prepared to switch the bombardment to the next objective. Then whistles blew, and the attack began.

Previous page: Rollcall of 1st Lancashire Fusiliers at Beaumont Hamel, 1 July 1916. This regular battalion also took part in the initial assault landing on Gallipoli in 1915, famously winning 'six VCs before breakfast'.

CHAPTER 2

THE FIRST DAY ON THE SOMME

FAILURE IN THE NORTH

At the northern extremity of the battlefield, two divisions of VII Corps, commanded by Lieutenant General Sir T. d'O Snow – inevitably if unoriginally known as 'Snowball' within the army – attacked around Gommecourt. This formation was part of Allenby's Third Army, and the purpose was to create a diversion while simultaneously ironing out an awkward German held bulge in the line. To this end, they were to advertise their preparations to the Germans. The plan was to the liking of neither general. Particularly worrying was the fact that a gap of 1 mile would be left between Third Army's southernmost formation and the northern flank of Fourth Army. It was rightly feared that the Germans would take advantage of this. The attack was entrusted to two territorial divisions. The left flank of Gommecourt was attacked by 46th (North Midland) Division (Major General E.J. Montagu-Stuart-Wortley), consisting of territorial battalions from the North and South Staffordshire, Lincolnshire and Sherwood Foresters regiments. Assaulting the right flank was 56th (London) Division (Major General C.P.A. Hull). This too was a TF formation, comprising veteran battalions, mainly from the London Regiment, with evocative names such as the Rangers, London Scottish and London Rifle Brigade.

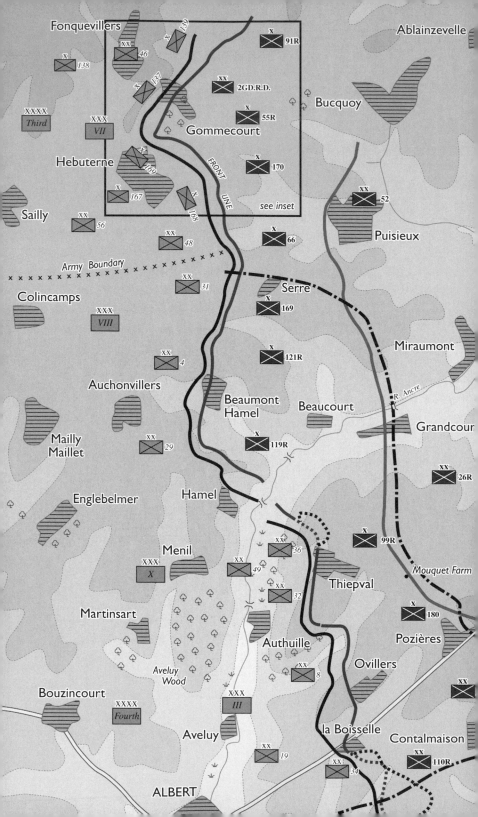

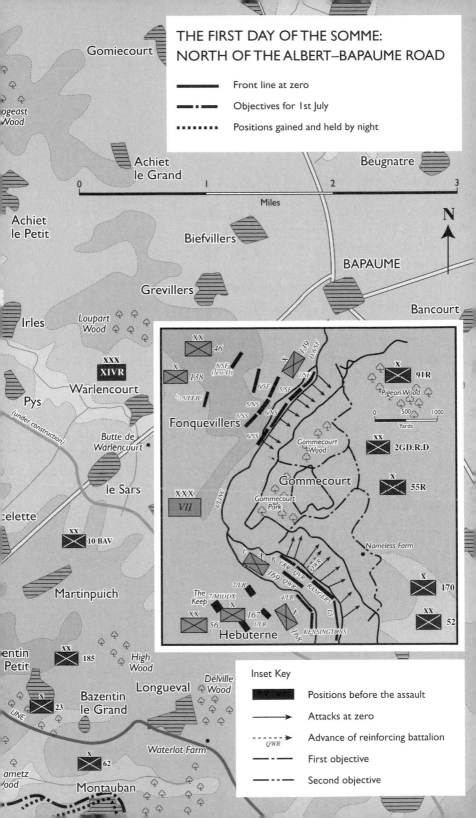

THE FIRST DAY OF THE SOMME:
NORTH OF THE ALBERT–BAPAUME ROAD

———————— Front line at zero

— · — · — Objectives for 1st July

· · · · · · · · Positions gained and held by night

Gomiecourt

Achiet
le Grand

Beugnatre

ogeast
Wood

Achiet
le Petit

Biefvillers

BAPAUME

N

0   1   2   3
Miles

Grevillers

Bancourt

Irles

Loupart
Wood

XXX
XIVR

Warlencourt

Pys
(under construction)

Butte de
Warlencourt

le Sars

celette

10 BAV

Martinpuich

XX 185

entin
Petit

High
Wood

X 23

LINE

Bazentin
le Grand

Longueval

Délville
Wood

X 62

Waterlot Farm

ametz
ood

Montauban

Inset

XX 46

8/SF (less D)

6/SF

X 138

0½5/LEIC

5/NS

5/SS

6/SS

Fonquevillers

XXX
VII

4/LINC

X 139

D. SF

7/SF

5/SF

6/NS

X 91R

Pigeon Wood

0   500   1000
Yards

Gommecourt
Wood

XX 2GD.R.D

Gommecourt

X 55R

Gommecourt
Park

Nameless Farm

L X R
169

LRB QVR
QVR RANGERS

X 170

The
Keep

2/LR

7/MIDDX

X 167

4/LR

KENSINGTONS

XX 52

XX 56

1/LR

1/68

Hebuterne

Inset Key

▨ Positions before the assault

——→ Attacks at zero

- - -→ Advance of reinforcing battalion
QVR

— · — First objective

— · · — Second objective

A sentry at Beaumont Hamel. One of Fourth Army's objectives on 1 July, it finally fell to 51st (Highland) Division as late as November.

Initially, the Londoners did well. Assembling in no man's land under the cover of a smoke-screen, they found that the German wire had been cut. The infantry pushed forward, overrunning the first two German trenches. Resistance stiffened once the third trench was reached, and Nameless Farm strongpoint held out stubbornly. 56th Division's undoing was the German artillery, which began to shell the British trenches and no man's land. Barrage is a French word that in 1916 had only recently entered the British military lexicon. Literally, it means a 'barrier', and that word described all too accurately what lay between the assaulting troops of 168 and 169 Brigades and their reserves. Starved of reinforcements, the Londoners could not hold on to their gains in the face of fierce counter-attacks from the German 2nd Guards Reserve Division. For all that, a party from the Queen's Westminster Rifles, commanded by Second Lieutenant G.S. Arthur, an officer of the Divisional Pioneer Battalion, 1/5 Cheshires, fought their way to the rear of Gommecourt, to where the rendezvous with the 46th Division should have taken place. Sadly, 46th Division never reached this point.

In contrast to the experience of 56th Division, the Midlanders' attack had been a disaster from the very beginning. They found the wire largely uncut, and the density of the British smoke barrage hampered rather than aided the assault. Isolated parties from 137 Brigade penetrated the German front line but made little progress, and German artillery and machine-guns caused heavy losses among the troops following up. 139 Brigade did better, but could not get into the second line in any strength. Having halted 46th Division's attack, the defenders of Gommecourt could turn their attention to the 56th, who were also exposed to fire from their 'open' flank, where no British troops were attacking. Second Lieutenant Arthur sacrificed his life in covering the retirement from the rendezvous. Despite fighting tenaciously to hold on to their gains, by 9.30 p.m. 56th Division had been driven back to the British trenches. 56th Division suffered 4,300 casualties. 46th Division's losses were lower – 2,455; in fact, these were the lowest losses of the thirteen British divisions that attacked as complete formations. Montague-Stuart-Wortley had refused to throw lives away by renewing the attacks, and there is little doubt that he was correct. None the less, he was 'stellenbosched' – sacked from his command – on 5 July. The Gommecourt attack had been an utter failure as a diversion or as anything else.

The troops that attacked on the extreme left flank of Fourth Army belonged to Major General R. Wanless O'Gowan's 31st Division, part of Lieutenant General Sir Aylmer Hunter-Weston's VIII Corps. This division was the Pals formation *par excellence*. Its order of battle featured Pals battalions from the industrial towns and cities of northern England: Bradford, Leeds, Barnsley, Durham, Halifax, Accrington; four battalions from Hull (Commercials, Tradesmen, Sportsmen and the aptly named T'Others); and the Sheffield City Battalion. Their part in the plan was quite complex. They were to capture the village of Serre, and to turn at right angles to the main line of advance to form a 'shoulder', which would protect against a German strike on Fourth Army's northern flank. Attacking uphill from a series of copses named after the writers of the Gospels, 93 and 94 Brigades immediately walked into heavy fire: 74,000 rounds of ammunition were expended by the defenders. 31st Division suffered terrible losses for very meagre gains. Elements of 18th DLI reached Pendant Copse, 1¼ miles from the British front line, and some men of the Accrington Pals and Sheffield City Battalion got as far as Serre village before they were killed or captured. Forty-five years after the war, a novelist wrote the epitaph of the Pals: 'Two years in the making. Ten minutes in the destroying.'[1] In all, the division lost 3,600 men. Like the diversion at Gommecourt, the attack on Serre achieved nothing of military value.

On the right of 31st Division, Hunter-Weston's corps made its first important gain when the regular 4th Division (Major General W. Lambton) captured the Quadrilateral Redoubt (known to the Germans as the 'Heidenkopf'). However, 4th Division was unable to capitalize on this success, not least because of the failures of both of the divisions on their flanks. Taking fire from Serre and Beaumont Hamel, 4th Division were unable to get further forward in any strength, and were subject to a number of ferocious counter-attacks. Such was the pressure on the British defenders of the Quadrilateral that on the morning of 2 July they abandoned it, recognizing that the position was indefensible. 4th Division's losses amounted to some 4,700.

The area around Beaumont Hamel is probably the best known to modern visitors to the battlefield. From the preserved trenches in the Newfoundland Memorial Park, one can look out over the area where 29th Division attacked on 1 July. Like the neighbouring 4th Division, Major General Beauvoir de Lisle's 29th Division was composed mainly of regular battalions. Nicknamed the 'Incomparable' Division, it had previously served in Gallipoli, where it had been commanded by Hunter-Weston, and 1 July marked its first major action on the Western Front. The 29th Division was to find that fighting the Germans on the Somme was a much tougher proposition than fighting the Turks at the Dardanelles, grim as that experience had been. A few weeks later at Pozières, the Australians were to make a similar discovery.

Many of the images most closely associated with the battle of the Somme come from 29th Division's attack at Beaumont Hamel on 1 July 1916. This is because Geoffrey Malins, one of only two official film cameramen, shot much footage on this sector. The resultant film, *The Battle of the Somme*, was a huge success. It is equally familiar today, excerpts having long been a staple of television documentaries. The German defences on 29th Division's front were formidably strong to begin with, the Redan Ridge dominating this part of the battlefield. The timing of the detonation of the mine at Hawthorn Redoubt made the job of the assaulting infantry even more difficult. This was a tunnel, reaching under the German positions, packed with 40,000 pounds of high explosive. Malins later recorded his impressions of the explosion:

> The ground where I stood gave a mighty convulsion. It rocked and swayed. I gripped hold of my tripod to steady myself. Then for all the world like a gigantic sponge, the earth rose high in the air to the height of hundreds of feet. Higher and higher it rose, and with a

horrible grinding roar the earth settles back upon itself, leaving in its place a mountain of smoke.

I swung my camera round onto our own parapets. Then another signal rang out, and from the trenches in front of me, our wonderful troops went over the top. What a picture it was![2]

The mine was blown at 7.20 a.m., ten minutes before zero hour, in the hope that the crater could be occupied before the main assault. Inevitably, this alerted the Germans, who put down heavy artillery and machine-gun fire on the British positions. The 2nd Royal Fusiliers sent two platoons of D Company to occupy the crater but had to contest it with German infantry, who held on to the far lip.

Malins's film was a record of almost complete failure. 87 and 86 Brigades, attacking at zero hour, were mostly cut down in no man's land, without even reaching the German front line. Sticking to pre-determined barrage plans, the British artillery pounded the second and third German lines, which the infantry ought to have reached. In reality, they were pinned down in front of the German first line. One of Malins's most enduring images is of a group of the 1st Lancashire Fusiliers, sheltering in a sunken lane out in no man's land. This position can readily be reached by modern visitors to the battlefield, and standing there it is not difficult to visualize the scenes of carnage as the Fusiliers attacked. Even the restrained language of the official history conveys something of the disaster: 'the Lancashire men were mown down directly they showed above the dip in which the lane lies.'[3]

Worse was to come. Few solid facts had emerged through the fog of war to reach General de Lisle. Misled by wildly inaccurate reports of the success of initial waves, he ordered forward his reserve formation, 88 Brigade. One of the battalions committed was 1st Newfoundland Regiment, the only unit recruited from outside the British Isles to attack on 1 July. Finding the forward trenches blocked with men and equipment, the Newfoundlanders clambered out into the open behind the British front line, and were almost immediately caught by German machine-gun fire. The Newfoundland Battalion lost numerous casualties even before it had reached no man's land, and a bare handful of men actually reached the German trenches. Today, a handsome bronze caribou, a fitting symbol of Newfoundland, then independent but today part of Canada, looks towards Y-Ravine, the German position from where the deadly fire came. The Newfoundlanders sustained 684 casualties, 91 per cent of the original force; a total exceeded on 1 July only by 10th West Yorkshires (17th (Northern) Division), who lost 710.[4] In all, the 'Incomparable' 29th Division's losses amounted to 5,240 men.

A few hundred yards from where the martyrdom of 29th Division was taking place, 36th (Ulster) Division won a spectacular victory, only to see most of its initial gains recaptured by the Germans. In the early summer of 1914, the British government had been concerned by the threat of war, but had feared that it would break out in Ireland, rather than France. Asquith's Liberal government was attempting to force through an Act that would give Home Rule, a form of devolved government, to Ireland. Many Protestants in the north were prepared to fight the forces of the Crown to prevent themselves from being ruled from Dublin. The Ulster Volunteer Force, armed with weapons from Germany, was raised to resist coercion by British troops. At the outbreak of the Great War in 1914, Lord Kitchener had accepted the offer of these partially trained and disciplined units for his New Armies, and they were converted into battalions of regular Irish regiments. They were certainly unusual formations. The soldiers were more than normally pious, and many were united by membership of Orange lodges. According to the old-style calendar, 1 July was the anniversary of the 1690 battle of the Boyne, a highly significant moment in Protestant Irish lore. Some men reputedly went into action wearing their Orange sashes, shouting, 'No Surrender!' Thus on 1 July 1916 men who had been drilling in preparation to fight the forces of the British Crown two years before, attacked the king's enemies near Thiepval.

36th Division, commanded by Major General O.S.W. Nugent, was part of Lieutenant General Sir T.N.L. Morland's X Corps. Unlike on some other divisional sectors, the Ulster Division was aided by effective artillery fire, including some French batteries. Under the cover of smoke shells fired by trench mortars, the infantry crawled out into no man's land ahead of zero hour. At 7.30 a.m. they won the race to the German parapet and rapidly captured the front line. Here the Ulsters faced a similar problem to that of 56th (London) Division at Gommecourt. 36th Division's assault might have been successful, but as we have seen, on their left the 29th Division was making minimal progress, as was 36th Division's own extreme left flank. On their right, 32nd Division made some headway, but far less than 36th Division. The further the Ulstermen advanced, the longer their exposed flanks became. The Germans were able to concentrate on this khaki salient jutting out into their positions. The Ulsters were thus being raked with fire from the front and both sides. Moreover, the Germans put down a heavy barrage on no man's land and the British trenches, effectively sealing off the assault troops. Although the 36th Division captured the key positions of Schwaben and Stuff Redoubts, since reinforcements could not reach them their numbers dwindled and they were pushed back from most of their initial gains. The day cost the Ulster Division losses of 5,104 men.

The high ground of the Thiepval plateau was one of the strongest parts of the German positions, eventually falling as late as 27 September. On 1 July it was the objective of 32nd Division, (Major General W.H. Rycroft), a New Army formation recruited from the north of England and Glasgow, its order of battle also including two regular battalions, 2nd King's Own Yorkshire Light Infantry (KOYLI) and 2nd Royal Inniskilling Fusiliers. It was, however, a Kitchener battalion, the Glasgow Commercials – more formally, 17th Highland Light Infantry (HLI) – that had the greatest success. Leaving their trenches at 7.23 a.m., the infantry moved to within 30 or 40 yards of the German position. Like the Ulsters to their left, the Glasgow Commercials got in among the German trench before the defenders could react and captured the Leipzig Redoubt. The HLI attempted to capitalize on their success, but once they left the shelter of the Leipzig Salient they came under heavy machine-gun fire from the Wonder Work, and were unable to get forward. Leipzig Redoubt was held after stiff fighting, but it proved to be 32nd Division's only gain.

The portion of the battlefield straddling the Albert–Bapaume road lay in the sector of Lieutenant General Sir W.P. Pulteney's III Corps. Major General H. Hudson's regular 8th Division was tasked with capturing the Ovillers spur, which lay to the north of the road. This formation had a particularly wide stretch of no man's land to cross, as much as 750 yards. The German trenches snaked back to take advantage of the spurs from the ridge, leaving the British only one approach, along the killing ground of Mash Valley. 8th Division's advance was enfiladed by the Thiepval Spur on the left and La Boisselle on the right, with Ovillers village 'a solid and terrible obstacle' directly to the front. Hudson chose to put all three of its brigades 'in the shop window', as it were, by attacking in line abreast.

In spite of the formidable handicaps imposed by the terrain, the men of 8th Division penetrated the German positions, albeit temporarily and at a fearful cost. On the right, 23 Brigade advanced up Mash Valley. About two hundred men of the two assault battalions, 2nd Middlesex and 2nd Devons, although raked with machine-gun fire, reached the German second trench. Forced back to the German front-line trench, about seventy men none the less held some 300 yards until 9.15 a.m., when they fell back into no man's land. In the centre, 25 Brigade too attacked the German second line until they were forced to fall back to the British positions. The left-hand formation, 70 Brigade, even managed to get a substantial group of men up to the German third trench. Once again, the ability of the Germans to impose a virtually impassable barrier of fire between the successful assault troops and the reserves on the wrong side of no man's land was critical.[5] Here as elsewhere co-operation between artillery and infantry was rudimentary. 'Our own artillery barrage had moved on to the divisional objective and the Heavy Artillery barrage had been lifted for

A German sentry of 127 Regiment using a trench periscope. This unit fought as part of 27th Division, which was in the line opposite the British on the Somme front.

The Hawthorne Mine detonates at 7.20am, 1 July 1916. Filmed by Geoffrey Malins, the explosion formed a vast crater that was the scene of a fierce struggle involving 29th Division.

over an hour from the valley. The German infantry and machine gunners… were able to remain in their trenches and take deliberate measures for defence.'[6]

It had been obvious from the beginning that 8th Division had been set a very difficult task. One battalion commander, Lieutenant Colonel E.T.F. Sandys (2nd Middlesex), had terrible forebodings about the attack, and aired his concerns to his superiors, to no effect. Sadly, his fears were all too justified. On 1 July his battalion suffered 540 casualties. Sandys was wounded in the attack and was unable to live with the memories. In September 1916, while recovering in London, he took his own life.[7]

On the right of 8th Division was a New Army formation, 34th Division (Major General E.C. Ingouville-Williams). 102 and 103 Brigades were extremely clannish Pals units, consisting as they did of battalions of the Northumberland Fusiliers, divided into Tyneside Irish and Tyneside Scottish, while 101 Brigade contained the 1st and 2nd Edinburgh City Battalions (15th and 16th Royal Scots), the Grimsby Chums (10th Lincolns) and the Cambridge Battalion (11th Suffolks). On the division's flanks, in Mash and Sausage Valleys, no man's land was hundreds of yards wide, but in the centre around the village of La Boisselle it narrowed to just a few yards. Here, in the 'Glory Hole', the front lines were 'in a constant state of flux... you might find yourself suddenly confronted by the muzzle of a Boche rifle poking through a loop hole in a sand-bag wall, newly built across the trench.'[8]

At 7.28 a.m. two mines were detonated under the German lines. Y-Sap mine, north of La Boisselle, contained 40,000 pounds of high explosive. The 60,000-pound Lochnagar mine, south of the village, left a crater 90 yards wide and 70 feet deep. Parties from the Grimsby Chums, Cambridgeshires, and 24th Northumberland Fusiliers (1st Tyneside Irish) got into the crater, but were unable to push on. The bulk of these battalions could not get across 500 yards of the bullet-swept no man's land to join them. Likewise, the Tyneside Scottish battalions of 102 Brigade took massive casualties as they crossed no man's land. The Tyneside Irish Brigade followed immediately behind the assault units, intending to pass through them and strike out for Contalmaison. Advancing from Tara and Usna Hills, they had to march about a mile in view of the Germans, and made excellent targets for machine-gunners, who effectively destroyed 103 Brigade before it had crossed the British front line. 34th Division's failure was nearly complete, but small parties of infantry pushed well beyond the German front line. One group from 16th Royal Scots actually reached Contalmaison before it was wiped out.

Today, the La Boisselle sector is one of the most visited areas of the Somme. The Lochnagar crater remains as a visible reminder of the events of 1 July, as does the shell-scarred area of the Glory Hole, while a handsome stone seat stands in mute testimony to the sacrifices of the Tyneside battalions. With 6,380 casualties on 1 July 1916, 34th Division's losses were the highest of any British division on that day; the two Tyneside brigades were promptly exchanged for two from 37th Division. General Ingouville-

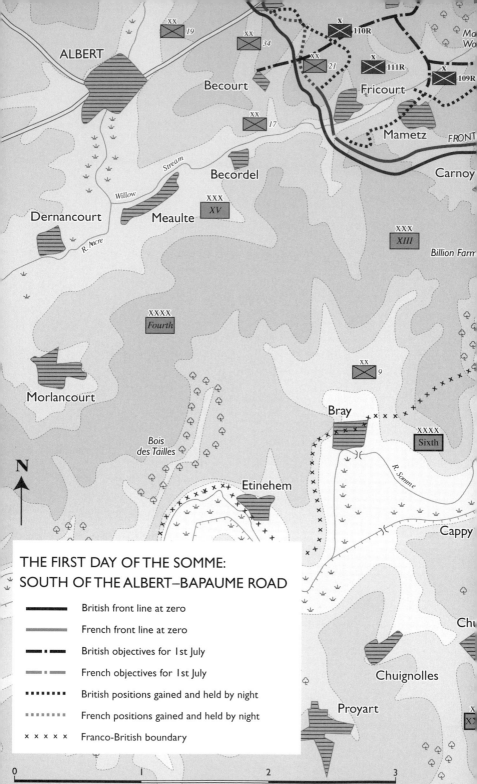

THE FIRST DAY OF THE SOMME:
SOUTH OF THE ALBERT–BAPAUME ROAD

British front line at zero

French front line at zero

British objectives for 1st July

French objectives for 1st July

British positions gained and held by night

French positions gained and held by night

Franco-British boundary

0   1   2   3

Miles

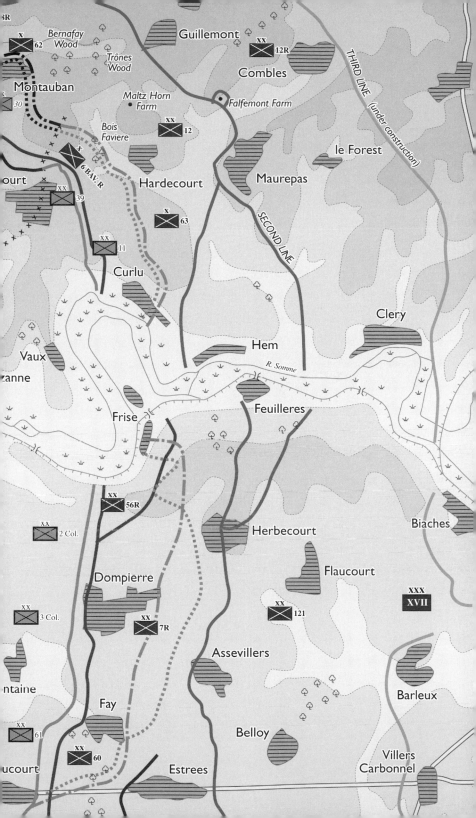

Williams – 'Inky Bill' to his men – survived this day but on 22 July he was killed by German shellfire while on a reconnaissance.

BRITISH SUCCESSES SOUTH OF THE BAPAUME ROAD

South of the Albert–Bapaume road, the situation was much more favourable. On terrain strikingly different from that in the area of the Ancre, British divisions had considerable success on 1 July, albeit at a heavy price in casualties.

One of Douglas Haig's protégés, Lieutenant General Henry Horne, commanded XV Corps. Like Haig, Horne was a Scot. A gunner, he belonged to the socially elite Royal Horse Artillery. Clearly, he enjoyed Haig's confidence, and by the end of the Somme campaign had been promoted to command First Army. Horne held this position, which he executed with some success, until the end of the war.

Horne attacked with two divisions in the line. The first, 21st Division, had a poor start to its career on the Western Front. A New Army formation with a high proportion of Yorkshire units, it had first seen action at Loos in September 1915. Committed to battle after a punishing approach march, 21st Division had been routed. The fault was not really that of the inexperienced Kitchener volunteers. The handling of the reserves at Loos by British high command became a *cause célèbre* that was largely responsible for costing Sir John French his job as C-in-C of the BEF. Despite this inauspicious start, 21st Division, with 50 Brigade (from 17th Division) under command, was one of the assault formations on 1 July. Its commander, Major General D.G.M. Campbell, was nicknamed 'Soarer' after the horse he had ridden to victory in the 1896 Grand National. Under Campbell's leadership, 21st Division was eventually to emerge as a formidable fighting formation.

At 7.28 a.m., mines were blown in the Tambour area. Although advancing troops suffered severely from fire from the villages of Tambour and Fricourt, parties reached and consolidated Crucifix Trench to the rear of Fricourt. One of the subalterns in 9th KOYLI was Lieutenant Basil Liddell Hart. In later years he was to become one of the fiercest critics of British high command, but at this stage he was still laudatory of his generals, his enthusiasm undimmed by the only partial success achieved by his division on 1 July, at the price of 4,256 casualties. One of the most bizarre episodes of the entire battle occurred on this sector. At 7.45 a.m. a company of 7th Green Howards attacked the German trenches, against orders and with no support. A German machine-gun team found itself with the perfect target. Military historians tend to use the word 'destroyed' rather loosely, but on this occasion it was all too apt.

The veteran 7th Division (Major General H.E. Watts) had served on the Western Front since 1914. Like the other divisions of the old army, it retained its essentially regular ethos despite having a number of New Army battalions in its order of battle. 22 Brigade attacked south of Fricourt, 20th Manchesters and 1st Royal Welch Fusiliers making some gains. But for all the damage inflicted on the British at Fricourt, the Germans too had suffered heavily. With elements of 21st Division in the rear of Fricourt, the village was clearly untenable, and the defenders began to pull out on the night of 1 – 2 July. Early on the 2nd a patrol of 8th North Staffordshires (17th Division) entered the village and took 100 prisoners. Thus Fricourt fell, a day later than planned.

Fricourt was not the first village to be captured by XV Corps, as on 1 July 7th Division had taken Mametz. On its right, 91 Brigade had attacked across 100 to 200 yards of no man's land, a distance that makes an interesting comparison with the 750 yards that 2nd Middlesex attempted to cross on 8th Division's sector. 20th Brigade also co-operated in capturing the village, and with the village taken, the assault troops pushed out on to the far side. Neither brigade had an easy time in reaching their objectives. Captain D.L. Martin, an officer of 9th Devons (20 Brigade) had previously constructed a terrain model from modelling clay, and realized that the 'Shrine' position posed a real threat to his battal-

Next page: British troops moving though Becourt Wood. As this photograph indicates, the BEF was a 'semi-modern' army with a mixture of horse-drawn and motor transport.

ion's advance. Sadly, he was proved correct, being killed by machine-gun fire from that very position. Another victim from this battalion was Lieutenant W.N. Hodgson. Shortly before the Somme began, Hodgson wrote one of the most moving of all poems to emerge from the Great War, 'Before Action', which ended with the plea, 'ere the sun swings his noonday sword ... Help me to die, O Lord'. His poem was prophetic. Hodgson was killed in the Devons' attack.

The capture of Mametz and Fricourt opened up real possibilities of a sustained advance against the battered German forces in the southern part of the British sector on the Somme. So did the most spectacular British gains of the first phase of the battle, made by XIII Corps (Lieutenant General Walter Congreve VC). When it was raised in 1914 there was little inkling that 18th (Eastern) Division would turn out to be an élite fighting formation. A Kitchener formation, its battalions lacked the obvious cohesion of the Pals units that comprised 30th Division, its neighbour on 1 July. An officer of one battalion of 18th Division, the 8th East Surreys, wrote an account of its training. His little book showed how a disparate group of civilians ('rather like a football excursion crowd', commented the regular adjutant[9]) gradually developed into a disciplined body of men. While this process was occurring simultaneously in hundreds of New Army units, 18th Division had a particular advantage, in that its commander was a first class trainer of men, perhaps the best in the British Army. This was Major General Ivor Maxse, a Guardsman who had commanded a brigade in the original BEF of 1914. Stamping his formidable personality on 18th Division, he was instrumental in turning it into one of the BEF's best trained divisions.

While the battalions of 18th Division were of regiments from southern England and East Anglia, the core of 30th Division comprised four battalions each of Liverpool and Manchester Pals, together with a scattering of regular units. 30th Division was a

The ability of the French army to participate in the Somme offensive while the Verdun fighting continued came as an unpleasant surprise to Falkenhayn. Here, a group of typical Poilus *occupy a trench.*

Journaux Rousselle, Pont-à-Mousson

remnant of feudal England. The 17th Earl of Derby, a territorial
and political magnate who dominated affairs in the north-west of
England, had a large hand in raising the Liverpool Pals (formally,
the 17th to 20th Battalions of the King's Liverpool Regiment or
'KLR'). His brother, the Hon. F.C. Stanley, commanded 89
Brigade, while another sibling, the Hon. G.F. Stanley, commanded
the guns of 149 Brigade Royal Field Artillery, both within
30th Division. Major General J.S.M. Shea had only taken over 30th
Division in May 1916. On 1 July the extreme right-hand battalion
of the division was 1st Liverpool Pals. The battalion's CO,
Lieutenant Colonel B.C. Fairfax, went over with the second wave,
linking arms with his opposite number in the left-hand French
unit, Commandant Le Petit of 3rd Battalion 153rd Regiment. Such
is the stuff of which legends are made. Regrettably, Anglo-French
relations at a higher level than that of battalion commander were
not always so amicable.[10]

By about 1.00 p.m. on 1 July, 30th Division had captured all of its
objectives, including the village of Montauban. A couple of hours
later, 18th Division had also completed its tasks. Success in this
sector was virtually complete, although at a high cost in casualties:
3,011 for 30th Division, 3,115 for 18th. XIII Corps had been helped
by the comparative weakness of German defences in this sector,
the use of a creeping barrage, and the powerful support of French
artillery. What is clear to the historian now, but not to GHQ then,
was that by the night of 1 July the diversion at Gommecourt had
failed in its primary and secondary purposes. North of the
Albert–Bapaume road, the attack had failed almost in its entirety.
The few territorial gains – in the Schwaben Redoubt and the
Leipzig Redoubt – were small compensation for the heavy casualties. South of the road, XV Corps had been more successful. XIII
Corps had taken all its objectives. So had the French.

The French contribution to the battle of the Somme was considerably smaller than envisaged at Chantilly, but none the less
significant. General Fayolle's Sixth Army (part of Foch's Northern
Group of Armies) deployed Balfourier's XX Corps north of the
River Somme, next to British XIII Corps. On the southern bank

was Berdoulat's I Colonial Corps and Jacquot's XXXV Corps. As on British XIII Corps' front, the German positions were far weaker than north of the Albert road, and the initial advance was aided by a river mist. South of the Somme, the eighty-four French heavy batteries overwhelmed the eight opposed to them. XX Corps achieved all of its objectives and was only prevented from going further by the fact that the British on their flank were not following up. In places, the Germans resisted fiercely. 39th Division (General Nourrisson) had a tough fight to clear Faviere Wood, on the boundary with British 30th Division, and the village of Curlu fell to General Vuillemot's 11th Division at the second attempt. Overall, the first day on the Somme was a considerable success for French XX Corps.

If anything, the forces south of the Somme did even better. Whereas XX Corps had attacked at the same time as the British, 7.30 a.m., the other two corps attacked a full two hours later, which gave them the advantage of surprise. I Colonial Corps took the villages of Dompierre and Becquincourt, and XXXV captured Fay, and had moved menacingly close to the German Second Position. Four thousand prisoners had been taken, and French losses were, by the standards of that dreadful day, light. No wonder that when Fayolle met Joffre that day, the C-in-C was beaming.[11]

Rawlinson failed to take advantage of the success of his southern flank. Perhaps he simply did not believe the messages that were reaching him indicating success. Certainly, problems of co-ordination and congestion along the Anglo-French boundary would have been real enough. Whatever the reasons, Rawlinson did not order the cavalry reserves, held to the north along the axis of the Albert road, to move to the south. Even the immediate operational reserve, 9th (Scottish) Division, was dispersed rather than concentrated for an immediate advance.

Even if Rawlinson missed the significance of events in the south, Haig did not. At 10.55 a.m., the C-in-C sent a telegram to his wife indicating that there had been considerable success in the area and that the cavalry might be pushed throughout the German positions. He was over-optimistic, but to consider the 'might-have-

A British 12-inch railway gun behind the lines at Meaulte. The lack of heavy guns hampered British operations on the Somme.

beens' is a painful process. The Germans south of the road had taken a terrible battering. To begin with their positions were significantly weaker than those further north. In all, the Germans lost 109 guns north of the River Somme. The defensive line from Longueval to Ovillers was a mere thing of shreds and patches. As late as 3 July an officer of Maxse's 18th Division took a reconnaissance party some 2 miles into German positions and came across no significant opposition. Terrain features for which the Germans would exact a terrible price in August and September were there for the taking. We know that by failing to capitalize on the success in the south the British commanders let an opportunity for a substantial advance go begging. Rawlinson never believed in Haig's plan for a breakthrough, and this probably influenced his reaction to events on XIII Corps' front. To lack any form of immediately deployable operational reserve was a mistake.

We should be careful, however, to keep the 'might-have-beens' in proportion. Even if the mobile reserve had been committed to exploit success on XIII Corps' sector, Haig's ambitious breakthrough plan was unlikely to have succeeded. Gough's cavalry-based force would not have been strong enough to reopen mobile warfare. The sheer exhaustion of the rest of Fourth Army would have militated against a major, war-winning advance. As we have seen, such was the immaturity of the BEF's logistic system that even if, against all the odds, a major breakthrough had occurred, it could not have been sustained. Fourth Army might have forced the Germans back some distance before supply problems forced it to halt, leaving Haig to prepare for another attritional campaign perhaps 20 miles forward of the old front line. This would have been far more significant as a political than a military victory.

On 1 July 1916 the BEF suffered 57,470 casualties. 19,240 were killed or died of wounds, 35,493 wounded, 2,152 missing and 585 taken prisoner. This was the bloodiest day in the history of the British Army. Perhaps 10,000–12,000 Germans became casualties. Why was the BEF's attack along much of its front such a disaster? An obvious conclusion was that the BEF was simply not up to the task that its commanders had set. Just over twenty-five months later, on ground just a few miles from the objectives of 1 July 1916, the BEF was to win a crushing victory over the Germans that resulted in an advance of 8 miles. The British, Australian and Canadian soldiers who attacked on 8 August 1918 were better armed and trained, and certainly more experienced, than their predecessors of 1 July 1916. In 1916 each 1,000-man infantry battalion deployed about four Lewis guns (light machine-guns) and perhaps two trench mortars. Battalions of August 1918 had only about half the manpower, but thirty Lewis guns and eight trench mortars. Tanks and aircraft supported the infantry and artillery fire was effective in a way that was just not possible on the first day on the Somme. Wireless (radio) communications, primitive as they were, gave a new dimension to command. In any case, commanders and staffs at all levels had benefited greatly from the experience of previous years. In short, in August 1918 the BEF had a finely tuned 'weapons system'. In July 1916 some of the weapons existed but there was scarcely a 'system' at all.

Many innovations had come about during the Somme offensive, or as a consequence of it. As we will see, tanks were introduced for the major push on 15 September 1916. The machine-gun barrage had its origins in 1915, but its first use on the Somme came in August 1916 at High Wood. The infantry platoon of 1 July consisted of four sections of riflemen. As a result of the experiences of the Somme, in February 1917 the platoon was restructured. Now it consisted of only one rifle section, plus one each of rifle bombers, bombers (hand-grenade throwers) and Lewis gunners. This basic organization proved highly flexible and effective, although it was further modified towards the end of the war. Many infantrymen attacked on 1 July carrying heavy kit. Within days, some units had adopted light fighting order, with subsequent waves of carrying parties to bring up sandbags, ammunition and the like.

The most striking advances came in the field of gunnery. The artillery plan for 1 July was deeply flawed. The lesson that many soldiers had learned from the battles of 1915 was that 'artillery conquers, infantry occupies'. The British official history argued that British commanders 'had relied on the bombardment destroying... [German] defences and ... morale ... their plan was framed, its tactics settled, and the troops trained in the sure and certain hope that the infantry would only have to walk over No Man's Land and take possession'.[12] Many commanders had a low opinion of the tactical ability of their troops, most of whom had been civilians eighteen months earlier, and thus used simple 'wave' formations to occupy the ground that was to have been 'conquered' by the artillery. As episodes throughout the Somme offensive were to demonstrate, citizen soldiers were capable of a much greater level of tactical sophistication than many had thought possible.

The 'artillery conquers, infantry occupies' concept suffered from a number of defects. Later in the war, artillery was indeed to prove a battle-winning weapon, but only within an all-arms team which created effective synergy. On 1 July 1916 the artillery and infantry conducted what amounted to separate battles. The artillery was supposed to shoot the infantry on to their objectives. However, with the gunners sticking to rigid timetables, too often the barrage raced ahead of the infantry pinned down in no man's land. The frailties of 1916-era communications made it very difficult to call the barrage back.

Even if co-operation between infantry and artillery had been near perfect, the attack would still probably have failed. Although the numbers of guns supporting the attack were greater than those assembled for any previous British battle, they were still too few for the task that Haig set.[13] Moreover, although the British counter-battery fire had done some damage, it failed to account for the 598 German field guns and 246 heavier pieces that the defenders were able to bring into action.

Modern visitors to the Somme will often see the evidence of the 'iron harvest': piles of unexploded shells lying beside the road or in the corners of fields. This gives a clue as to another problem facing the British gunners in July 1916: the inadequacies of their ammunition. Britain's creation of a war economy capable of sustaining a total war effort was a remarkable national achievement, as was a similar process in the USA, which provided much of the British Army's munitions. The cost in the short term was a diminution in

An artillery observation post near Flers, October 1916. British artillery techniques became increasingly sophisticated over the course of the 1916 campaign.

the quality of some products, shells and fuses among them. Moreover, about two-thirds of the $1^1/2$ million shells fired before the attack were shrapnel, lethal against exposed infantry but ineffective against men sheltering in dug-outs deep beneath the surface. The high explosive essential for this task was in chronically short supply. Not until 1917 would the supply of munitions catch up with the demand. Moreover, shell fuses were unreliable, frequently falling off while the shell was in the air or failing to ignite on impact, perhaps becoming buried in soft ground. Much improved versions were to reach the British gunners in the later part of the war, including the 106 graze fuse which greatly simplified the job of cutting barbed wire by artillery fire.

Effectiveness of artillery fire helps explain why the French attack was so much more successful than the British on 1 July. Fayolle's troops had a tenfold advantage in guns over the German defenders. The support of French guns may also have given 36th Division a crucial advantage in their attack near Thiepval, and XV and XIII Corps in the south also benefited from the support, either direct or indirect, of French artillery. While a reasonably competent (by 1916 standards) infantryman could be trained up in a matter of months, it took longer to turn a civilian into a gunner. In industrial terms, at the beginning of the Somme an infantryman was a semi-skilled worker (who would however acquire more technical expertise as the war went on). The artilleryman was a craftsman, who required a lengthy apprenticeship. Many of the techniques that were to make artillery so effective in 1917–18 – use of accurate meteorological information, sound-ranging, flash spotting – were in their infancy in July 1916. One technique that at least some formations used – 18th and 30th Divisions in XIII Corps among them – was a creeping barrage, a curtain of shells moving ahead of the infantry at the rate of perhaps 100 yards in three to five minutes. Far more effective than the clumsy artillery 'lifts' from objective to objective, this helps to explain the success in the south. By 1918 much had changed. During the battle of the Somme it was clear that artillery, firing in great depth, and airpower had changed the way war was conducted. By 1918 this change had gone much further, to the extent that it is fair to describe it as a revolution in military affairs. Indeed, it has been persuasively argued that this emergence of the modern style of warfare was the most important military development of the twentieth century, and everything that has come since has simply been a variation on this basic theme.[14]

A tactical instruction pamphlet, *Fourth Army Tactical Notes*, has entered Somme mythology as the reason why the infantry marched very slowly towards the enemy, presenting perfect targets to German machine-gunners. Both Haig and Rawlinson adhered, at least in this instance, to a 'hands-off' style of command, in that higher commanders set broad objectives but did not interfere with tactical detail. The problem was that this left the inexperienced Fourth Army formations in a 'tactical vacuum'.[15] Rawlinson's *Notes* were not prescriptive. They, and other documents, offered advice, much of it sound. Units did adapt tactics to suit the ground and other circumstances. Indeed, one historian has argued persuasively that when Edmonds, the British official historian, contrasted the clumsy 'wave' tactics with 'infiltration' methods, pushing small groups of infantry through weak spots in the enemy line, he was being thoroughly misleading. The BEF had, however imperfectly, grasped the essence of 'modern assault tactics' before the Somme began.[16] The problem lay in the execution, not doctrinal weakness.

If, as originally intended, the French Army had played the major role in the Somme offensive, would the first day have been more successful? The likelihood is that it would have been, but that it would still have fallen short of a breakthrough. In July 1916 the French Army was tactically more experienced and, crucially, had more heavy guns than the BEF. Foch had no faith in a quick breakthrough, and his preference for methodical reduction of the German defences was probably more suitable than Haig's more ambitious plan. Joffre's and Foch's understanding of the importance of co-ordinated attacks across a broad front also suggests that French generalship would have been superior to British. Even so, the strength of the German defences north of the Albert–Bapaume road would have proved a stern test for the French Army. The best hope for a substantial victory lay in success in the relatively weakly held southern sector, from the road to the River Somme. Perhaps the French might have made rather more of their opportunities than the BEF did in reality.

The 'First Day on the Somme' is so embedded in the British national consciousness that it is sometimes difficult to look beyond it to the rest of the campaign. Peter Simkins has rightly referred to the 'tyrannical hold' exercised on historiography and popular memory alike by 1 July.[17] In that I have devoted a disproportionate amount of space to one day out of a 141-day campaign this book has failed to break free of this tyranny. Yet that day did mark a significant phase in the battle. The next attack of comparable scope did not occur until 15 September, and the results of the first day on the Somme were far from negligible. As German high command clearly recognized, it caused them to lose the strategic initiative.

CHAPTER 3

THE SECOND PHASE: July 1916

ANGLO-FRENCH DISPUTES ON STRATEGY

There was no possibility of Haig calling off the offensive after the setbacks of 1 July, the battle having already developed a momentum of its own. It would not be difficult to imagine the reaction of a French high command, still coping with the trials of Verdun, to a proposal by the British to call off the battle after one day. The other members of the coalition – the Russians and the Italians – also had the right to expect the British would stick to the terms of the Chantilly agreement. Haig was determined to continue to fight, but on his own terms. At a meeting between Joffre and Haig on 3 July there was a volcanic argument. The Frenchman insisted that the BEF renew its assaults north of the Bapaume road. Haig stiffly resisted, resenting the attempt by the Frenchman to treat him as a subordinate, and holding firm to his idea that the BEF should capitalize on its gains in the southern sector. The fog of war was such that Haig and Rawlinson did not become aware of the scale of the losses on 1 July for several days. Even then, there was a generally held air of optimism in British high command that, if the Allies kept up the pressure, the German line would crack. Evidence from the German side of the lines (see below) suggests that this view was exaggerated, but not ridiculously so. The bottom line was that on 2 July 1916 the German Army was still occupying French and

Belgian territory, and in the absence of any compromise, only the application of violence by the Allies was likely to remove them. The dispute between Joffre and Haig on strategy had serious implications that greatly hampered the conduct of a 'joined-up', combined Anglo-French campaign. A basic problem was that whereas Haig believed in keeping constant pressure on the enemy, Foch and Joffre were prepared to suspend operations to ensure that the next blow was delivered in great strength. Joffre later argued that by August the BEF's efforts had 'little by little', degenerated 'into a series of disconnected actions, both costly and unprofitable'.[1] He thought that Haig was too willing to spend time straightening the line, mounting local attacks to eliminate outposts prior to a major attack, leading too often to the main operation being delayed. It was, he felt, a severe case of the tail wagging the dog. There is much truth in Joffre's criticisms. On the period 3 to 13 July, Fourth Army units were thrown, often in 'penny packets with inadequate artillery preparation' into no fewer than forty-six actions, which resulted in some 25,000 British casualties. Rawlinson's 'hands-off' approach to command had some virtues, but he can fairly be criticized for failing to ensure proper co-ordination between Fourth Army's corps.[2] In turn Haig cannot escape blame for failing to force Rawlinson to fight Fourth Army as an army, rather than as a disparate collection of units.

TOWARDS THE DAWN ATTACK

At 10.00 p.m. on 1 July, Rawlinson sent out orders to renew the attack. Haig recognized that, as it existed, Fourth Army's frontage was too big to be controlled by one man and, perhaps disappointed by Rawlinson's performance, he wished to bring his protégé Gough into the battle. The C-in-C thus appointed Gough to take control of X and VIII Corps; later this was formalized when Reserve Army assumed control of operations in the northern sector of the battlefield. Gough wisely reported that the state of confusion in his area was such that no operations could be carried out until 3 July. In the early hours of 2 July, a German counter-attack on Montauban was

Coalition warfare is conducted by means of committees and meetings.
Here, left to right, Joffre, Haig and Foch emerge from a meeting at Beauquesne
on 12 August 1916.

destroyed by XIII Corps with the aid of artillery. Fricourt fell on 2
July, and La Boisselle was attacked by 19th Division, after a feint
'Chinese' barrage against Ovillers. La Boisselle was cleared on 3
July. Attacks on 3 July by 12th Division against Ovillers, and 32nd
Division against the Leipzig Salient at Thiepval were failures. On
the southern flank, XV Corps failed to take the best advantage of
the enemy's weakness and confusion. Patrols found that Mametz
Wood and Quadrangle Trench were unoccupied, but by 4 July,
when efforts were made in earnest to secure the positions, the
Germans had put troops into Mametz Wood. 9th (Scottish)
Division of XIII Corps occupied Bernafay Wood on 3 July, and
Caterpillar Wood on the following day.

After Haig's meeting with Joffre, it was decided that the next
objective would be the German Second Position between Longueval and Bazentin le Petit. Fourth Army was to work its way forward
to a jumping-off position for the attack, while Gough's army was

mostly to confine its activities to operations to pin enemy forces to its front.

The lack of drive on XV and XII Corps' front on 2–3 July in part stemmed from the need to consult with French commanders, whose troops were operating on their immediate right; and from the fear of creating a vulnerable salient. But the British commanders must bear their share of the blame. In a strange reversal of positions held before the battle, Rawlinson was now in favour of getting 'through the German reserves and lines of defence as quickly as possible', while Haig stressed a more methodical course, emphasizing the importance of capturing Mametz Wood. In the event, the confusion of direction from high command led to delay and piecemeal attacks; as Clive Hughes has noted: 'lack of continuity in British operations more than anything else gave the Germans ample opportunity to mend their broken defences and bring forward their reserves.' Fourth Army could have secured some objectives at little cost at this stage that would only be taken after heavy fighting in the weeks to come, for the Germans were to make excellent use of the woods in this part of the battlefield as defensive positions. Rawlinson himself wrote in August that 'These four days would in all probability have enabled us to gain full possession of the hostile third line of defence, which was at that time less than half finished… It makes me sick to think of the "might have beens".'[3]

Fourth Army carried out a number of smallish-scale but bloody actions. On 7 July 17th (Northern) and 38th (Welsh) Divisions attacked in the Contalmaison–Mametz Wood area without success, while 12th and 25th Divisions made gains at Ovillers, although the ruins of the village were not finally to fall into British hands until 15–16 July. The 10th was marked by the capture of Contalmaison by 23rd Division, and Mametz Wood by 38th Division, at their second attempt. The fall of this sector at last brought Fourth Army within striking distance of the Longueval Ridge. The date for the attack was eventually fixed as Bastille Day, 14 July 1916.

THE INCOMPLETE VICTORY: 14 JULY 1916

Rawlinson and Congreve, the XIII Corps commander, devised a plan that was daringly different from that of 1 July. It involved simultaneous attacks by XV and XIII Corps, side by side, an assembly of troops under the cover of darkness, followed by the attack going in at dawn. The infantry would be heralded by an intense bombardment of only five minutes: unlike 1 July, surprise was of the essence. Initially, Haig was sceptical, believing that the plan, especially the approach march at night, demanded too much of the largely New Army troops who were to carry it out. Haig proposed his own, ironically quite complicated plan, a narrow front attack by XV Corps out of Mametz Wood followed by a turn east in the direction of Longueval; XIII Corps were to assault in a follow-up operation. After considerable debate between Haig, Rawlinson and the relevant corps commanders, Horne and Congreve, Rawlinson's plan gained approval. However, at Haig's insistence, 18th Division was given the preliminary tasks of capturing Trônes Wood on the right flank, and 1st Division was to form a defensive flank; and, quite properly, Rawlinson was ordered to pay more attention to counter-battery fire.

The attack was hugely successful. Although the artillery preparation commenced on 11 July, the British still achieved surprise. The artillery bombardment began at 3.20 a.m., and the infantry attack went in five minutes later. Faced by 1,200 yards of no man's land, the assaulting battalions of 7th Division pushed up to within 300–500 yards of the German positions, and began to creep forward:

> The last moments of this stealthy crawl were tense with excitement. Every minute that passed without detection saw the silent lines of crawling men steadily nearing their objective, every second meant a foot gained. At last the silent British guns suddenly roared off together, and as the barrage came hurtling down on the German trenches [2nd] Borders and [8th] Devons sprang to their feet with the leading lines only 100 yards away and rushed forward, entering

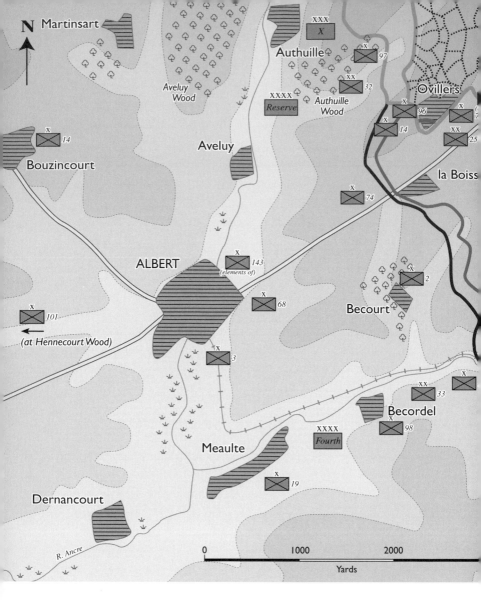

N

Martinsart

Aveluy
Wood

Authuille

```
XXX
X
```

```
X    97
```

```
XX    32
```

Ovillers

```
XXXX
Reserve
```

Authuille
Wood

```
X    96
```

```
X    14
```

```
X    7
```

```
X    14
```

Bouzincourt

```
XX    25
```

la Boiss

```
X    74
```

ALBERT

```
X    143
(elements of)
```

```
X    68
```

```
X    2
```

Becourt

```
X    101
```

(at Hennecourt Wood)

```
X    3
```

```
X
```

```
XX    33
```

Becordel

```
X    98
```

Meaulte

```
XXXX
Fourth
```

```
X    19
```

Dernancourt

R. Ancre

```
0        1000        2000
```

Yards

THE DAWN ATTACK ON 14TH JULY

——— British front line, 13/14th July	
——— Front of the Position of Deployment	– – – British front line, 1st July
——— Line gained, 14th July	–·–·– German front line, 1st July
·········· Trenches	x x x x x Franco-British boundary

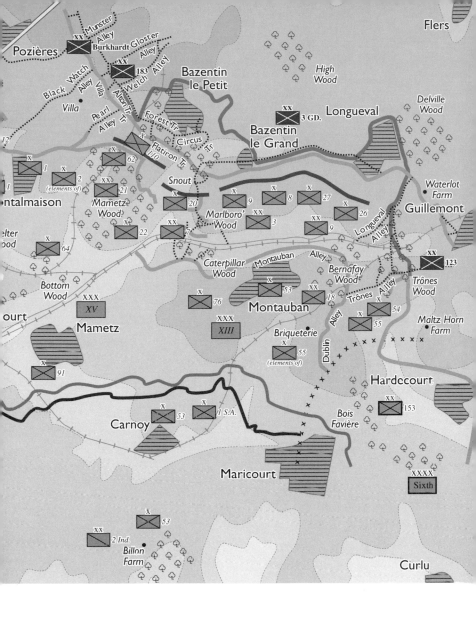

the enemy's position just as the barrage lifted onto the second line and almost before the Germans knew they were coming. The surprise had come off completely and the wire had been so admirably cut that it presented no obstacle, while the German trenches were full of dead, victims of the bombardment.[4]

7th Division took all their objectives. Similar methods were employed by the formation on either flank, 21st Division on the right and 3rd Division on the left, with comparable results. The right hand formation of the attack proper, 9th (Scottish) Division, fought their way into the fringe of Delville Wood, although they were unable to capture Waterlot Farm (actually a sugar refinery). On the right flank, in a subsidiary operation, 18th Division captured Trônes Wood. In all, some 6,000 yards of the German Second Position were in British hands by mid morning.

The potential for a major advance, and the eventual disappointment, is captured by a letter written by an officer on 7th Division's staff while the battle was in progress:

> 6 a.m. We started again this morning at 25 minutes past 3 – We are attacking Bazentin le Grand Wood & Bazentin le Petit Village and up to the present things seem to be going quite satisfactorily. I hope that by 9 o'clock we shall have got the Village. We have got the Wood already & a good many prisoners are coming back we hear. That is a good sign as if prisoners come in fairly freely, it means less hard fighting, less casualties & quicker progress. I am writing in a Dug Out a little bit behind our original frontline on and about 3 miles behind the infantry. We have cavalry close up & hope to be able to get to the enemy's third & last line of defence at Flers & Le Sars (not a strong line by tonight).
>
> 7.40 a.m. Things are going very well indeed, our infantry are pushing through the village, & I hope to hear in an hour's time that they have got it.
>
> 9.15 a.m. I really believe that we may be in for a big thing. I have been busy for the last hour & half getting things ready behind for a further advance & we captured all we were ordered to take very soon after I wrote my last sentence. We have got le Petit (Bazentin).

The people on our right have got Bazentin le Grand & Longueval & now some Cavalry are streaming past within 200 yards of the Dug Out & go through to try to reach the next German line. It is of course a bit of a gamble but may come off. I rushed out of my Dug Out & the General rushed out too & has stayed out. I have come back in case anything happens, but I don't think anything will happen for a bit now.

6.45 p.m. Not had a moment since I last wrote and the post is just off. We have not managed to accomplish much more today although things looked very rosy to start with & the attack is going on now. I think I will not post this tonight but just send a Post Card.

15 July... Things did not go as rapidly as I hoped at one time yesterday but we had a good day. [5]

The battle of 14 July was a remarkable but tantalizingly incomplete victory which seems to have taken the French as much by surprise as it had the Germans. One French commander had previously described it as 'an attack organized for amateurs by amateurs'. The effective use of artillery helps to explain reasons for the success. On 1 July the British had shelled 22,000 yards of front and 300,000 yards of trench behind the front line. A fortnight later, the comparative figures were 6,000 and 12,000 yards. On 14 July Rawlinson had two-thirds of the guns used on the first day on the Somme, but they were used to shell just over 5 per cent of the ground. Every yard of German trench was subjected to 660 pounds of shell, 'an intensity of fire ... five times that achieved before the 1 July attack'.[6] Combined with the achievement of surprise and sensible infantry tactics, artillery provided the key to the seizure of Bazentin Ridge.

The successful assault threw the Germans into confusion. The situation approximated to the one they faced on this sector on 1 July. Yet for the second time Rawlinson failed to take full advantage of initial success. His plan called for 2nd Indian Cavalry Division to exploit the infantry's gains, possibly because Rawlinson was aware of Haig's displeasure at his lack of enthusiasm for the use of cavalry in the planning for 1 July. The Fourth Army commander

The Deccan Horse near Carnoy, 14 July 1916. The fighting of this day demonstrated that under some circumstances horsed cavalry still had a place on the battlefield.

held the infantry back from pushing into High Wood, which was only lightly defended.

The use of cavalry was not necessarily a mistake. British cavalry-men were as adept at fighting on foot as from the saddle, and under the right conditions their mobility was a great asset. The problem was that it took an inordinate amount of time to pick their way through the trenches and shattered landscape before they reached the newly captured ground, which was relatively good going for cavalry. Summoned forward at 7.40 a.m., the 7th Dragoon Guards and 2nd Deccan Horse did not get into position for an advance until early evening. At 12.15 p.m. Rawlinson had ordered 7th

Division to move on High Wood, but this instruction was counter-manded by Horne of XV Corps, because possession of Longueval, which would have lain on the flank of the advance, was still being disputed. When the cavalry finally did attack, it achieved some success. The Dragoon Guards, lances couched, charged German infantry and machine-gunners hiding in crops and took thirty-two prisoners. Cavalry machine-gunners accounted for a German machine-gun, and two battalions of 7th Division attacked and captured the southernmost corner of High Wood.

Cavalry of the First World War can be likened to paratroops in the Second. In September 1944 lightly equipped airborne forces were dropped to seize the river crossings up to and across the Rhine, while XXX Corps attempted to link up on the ground. In the right circumstances, Great War cavalry were able to use their superior mobility to seize key ground 1,000 yards or so ahead of the main body. At High Wood, the cavalry deployed as infantry, but when support failed to arrive they fell back. If a larger body of cavalry had been available for prompt exploitation, and an infantry force had been able to link up with it, it is plausible that the British might have advanced 2,500 yards or so from Bazentin Ridge. This would not have created a breakthrough, but it would have taken them to the rear of Delville Wood and Longueval.[7] Such an attempt might have failed, but given the appalling casualties sustained in the battles to take these objectives over the next two months, it was surely a risk worth taking.

Ultimately, 14 July was something of a false dawn. The hope engendered by the capture of Bazentin Ridge fizzled out in attri-tional struggles for High and Delville Woods. Yet it demonstrated that Kitchener's Armies were capable of greater tactical sophisti-cation than some senior commanders had believed possible. The battle also demonstrated that artillery, used correctly, was a battle-winning weapon. It was not simply a matter of amassing large numbers of guns, but of employing them correctly as part of a coherent all-arms team. Unfortunately, the next couple of months were to show that these lessons had been imperfectly learned.

FRENCH OPERATIONS IN JULY 1916

South of the Somme, French troops made steady gains in the days following the initial attack. I Colonial Corps, whose divisional commanders seem to have been given considerable freedom of action by Berdoulat, got through the German Second Position on 2 July and was getting tantalizingly close to the town of Péronne. 'Foch felt that for the moment his chief function was to support the British, and with the resources at his disposal he could not do so and at the same time develop his action on the right.'[8] Fayolle noted in his diary on 3 July, the day that I Colonial Corps captured Flaucourt, taking many prisoners and guns, that the French should 'cover the Somme and hammer the south'. But to do this was impossible, because left alone, the British would do nothing. This was the perspective, however unfair, of the commander of a successful army who felt that he was being held back by ineffective allies.[9] If more forces had been available south of the Somme, even greater success might have been gained, given the weakness of the defences in that area and the initial confusion in German high command. But the moment passed, and more defenders arrived. By 14 July Sixth Army's progress south of the Somme had slowed to a crawl, and although there were some subsequent advances, Fayolle's dreams of a breakthrough had vanished.

GERMAN REACTIONS

At nightfall on 1 July, the German operational commanders on the Somme could not look to the immediate future with much optimism. Their troops had already endured seven days of heavy shelling before the attack had begun. Although they had repulsed the northern attack, the southernmost British units and the French had made steady progress, with the promise of more to come. The Germans lost 109 guns in the sector opposite the British; already heavily outgunned, this had serious consequences for their defence. Von Below on 4 July noted that he had only one battery in place every 800 metres; the experience of Verdun suggested that

'I'm watching and fighting for you. Sign up for the War Loan'. In a total war, propaganda played an important role in mobilising the civilian population.

one every 200 metres was desirable. Desperate measures were put into place to shore up the battered sections of the line in the southern part of the battlefield as newly arrived reserves were fed piecemeal into the fighting.

Historian John Terraine has rightly pointed out that 'the true texture of the Somme' consisted of German counter-attacks to retake lost territory as well as the initial British assaults. He identified at least 330 German counter-attacks during the Battle of the Somme. The inspiration for this policy came from the top. The commander of XVII Corps holding the sector south of the River Somme, General von Pannewitz, on 2 July ordered the abandoning of territory to shorten his line and prepare to counter-attack. Not only did this risk uncovering the flank of forces north of the Somme, it ran counter to Falkenhayn's instructions that 'it is a principle in trench warfare not to abandon a foot of ground and, if a foot is lost, to put in the last man to recover it by an immediate counter-attack.' Von Below shared these views, declaring that 'the enemy should have to carve his way over heaps of corpses.' Falkenhayn sacked Second Army's Chief of Staff and replaced him with Colonel von Lossberg, a specialist in defensive warfare. Ironically, Lossberg was to be influential in moving away from the policy of *Halten, was zu halten ist* or 'hold on to whatever can be held'.

As the reports of the ferocity of the Somme offensive began to reach Falkenhayn, he seems to have realized that he had miscalculated Second Army's ability to hold out, and thus buy time for a major counter-stroke using Rupprecht's Sixth Army. 'On average,' a German military commentator later stated, '1 German division held 7 to 8 kilometres, against which the enemy brought 3 to 4 divisions.' [10] Certainly, seven German divisions were on their way to the Somme by 2 July, and a further seven by 9 July. In all, forty-two extra German divisions were sent to the Somme during July and August. Thirty-five of them were put into the line opposite Fourth and Reserve Armies – tangible evidence that the BEF was pulling its military weight within the coalition. A new command and control structure had to be devised to handle the greatly inflated German order of battle. On 19 July forces north of the River Somme were reorganized as First Army, under von Below. The front south of the river came under the command of Second Army. The commander of this Army was General Max von Gallwitz (1852–1937), an artilleryman who had distinguished himself on the Eastern Front in 1915 and who had commanded at Verdun. Gallwitz also served as the commander of the Army Group formed by First and Second Armies.

Faced with the crisis on the Somme, on 11–12 July, Falkenhayn suspended major offensive operations at Verdun – this was a major strategic achievement of the Allied offensive. Germany simply had too few divisions to do everything that Falkenhayn had planned. The formations sent to the Somme were withdrawn from *Oberste Heeresleitung* (OHL – roughly the equivalent of British GHQ) reserve and Sixth Army; OHL had only one reserve division at its disposal by the end of August 1916. The major counterstroke in the West was quietly dropped in favour of holding firm on the Somme, hoping that this would persuade the French to come to terms with Germany. This, too, was a sign that the Franco-British offensive on the Somme had wrested the strategic initiative from Germany. [11]

THE BATTLE FOR THE WOODS

By 15 July German reinforcements had arrived to thicken the line opposite the Bazentin Ridge sector, and a fierce battle was developing in the Delville Wood area. 9th Division captured Waterlot Farm although it was not firmly held until 17 July. The South African Brigade of 9th Division captured most of Delville Wood in a two-stage attack. This established a pattern that was to be repeated several times during the two-month battle for 'Devil's Wood': successful attackers would face the problem of massive shelling – from several sides, since Delville Wood jutted out as a salient – and heavy German counter-attacks. The fighting for Delville and Longueval involved the 'Jocks' and 'Springboks' of 9th (Scottish) Division in a seesaw battle. The division was pulled out of action by 20 July, but

The shattered remains of Delville Wood, 20 September 1916.
The Germans made skilful use of woods to frustrate Fourth
Army's advance in the southern sector.

the battle was far from over. 3rd Division and a brigade of 18th Division had by this time taken its place in the line, and the fighting continued along much the same lines.

The fight for Delville was paralleled by the struggle at High Wood. 33rd Division attacked High Wood and the adjacent Switch Line on 15 July, without much success. The division renewed its attacks on 20 July, while 5th and 7th Divisions assaulted German positions to the east of High Wood. 33rd Division, which sported a divisional sign of a double three domino, captured part of the wood, but the fighting bogged down in stalemate. Away on the extreme right flank, 35th Division (a 'Bantam' formation of men below the usual height for enlistment) attacked near Maltz Horn Farm, without much success. On that day the French attacked on both banks of the River Somme, gaining some ground to the east of Hardecourt.

With the exception of the attack on 14 July, the fighting since the first day of the battle had been piecemeal and very often small scale. 35th Division's attack on 20 July, for example, had been conducted by just two companies of 15th Sherwood Foresters. Indeed, as Robin Prior and Trevor Wilson have pointed out, in the sixty-two days from 15 July to 14 September, 'Fourth Army carried out some 90 operations (attacks by at least one battalion), only four of which were launched across the whole of its front'. In this period about 82,000 casualties were incurred by Fourth Army for the capture of 1,000 yards on a 5-mile front. Less ground had been gained, for losses that were 40 per cent greater, than on 1 July.[12]

Rawlinson on 18 July had ordered a larger scale, multi-divisional attack between Guillemont in the east (on the boundary with the French) and Pozières, on the Roman road. The attack was eventually delivered on the night of 22–23 July. 30th Division attacked at Guillemont, 3rd Division at Delville Wood, 5th Division on their flank, 51st (Highland) Division at High Wood, 19th Division near Bazentin-le-Petit, and 1st Division between this village and Pozières. These attacking divisions made no progress and lost a number of men in the process. Two of these formations, 30th and 19th, had done well in earlier phases of the

Men of 2nd Australian Division resting near Becourt Wood, September 1916.
This division had a difficult Western Front debut on the Somme, but by 1918 had
emerged as an élite formation.

battle, and another, 51st, was to acquire a reputation as an élite division. The quality of the troops was not at fault.

What was wrong was that the night attack of 22–23 July was poorly co-ordinated. The French on 22 July had told Fourth Army that they would not be ready to attack, but Rawlinson misguidedly decided to go ahead in any case. The attacks by the British divisions started at four separate times, which reduced the synergy of the assault. During the victorious Hundred Days campaign of 1918 individual divisions within a corps were frequently able to attack at different times without adverse effect, but that was a vastly more experienced and capable force than the army of July 1916. Moreover, on 22–23 July the artillery preparation was

inadequate – in part because poor weather had limited the useful-
ness of the RFC in 'spotting' for the artillery, more essential than
ever because the German position was on a reverse slope. However,
in 30th Division's sector, the British gunners had a decent view over
the German trenches, which the Royal Artillery proceeded to
wreck. This did little to aid the attacking infantry, because the
Germans had moved towards a more flexible form of defence,
partly forsaking easily identifiable trenches, which made good
targets, for dispersed positions such as shell holes, which did not.
This meant that to be certain of suppressing the defenders' fire –
because as the Somme demonstrated time after time, one surviving
machine gun could cause havoc – the British gunners had to
expend a prodigious quantity of shells over a wide area. In 1918
such volumes of munitions were available. In 1916, when divisions
at Ypres had to economize on their expenditure of shells in order to
feed the fighting on the Somme, this was not the case.

THE AUSTRALIANS AT POZIÈRES

Gough's Reserve Army, rather than Rawlinson's Fourth, achieved
the one solid gain of the day: the capture of Pozières, which had
been the objective of four unsuccessful attacks prior to 23 July.
Jumping off at dawn, 48th (South Midland) Division made some
gains to the left of the Roman road, but it was 1st Australian
Division that struck the major blow, capturing Pozières village and
advancing 1,000 yards.

The Australian forces had only arrived from the Middle East in
March 1916. During the 1915 Gallipoli campaign the Australian
and New Zealand Army Corps had earned an impressive reputation as fighting troops, adding the word 'Anzac' to the English
language. The first Australian formation to fight in a major action
on the Western Front was 5th Division. On 19 and 20 July this division fought alongside British 61st Division at Fromelles near the
1915 Neuve Chapelle battlefield. Intended as a diversionary operation in parallel with the Somme, it was a bloody failure. Fromelles
further damaged Australian faith in British generalship, already

shaken after Gallipoli. Pozières was to make the situation even worse.

The importance of the village of Pozières lies in the fact that it was situated as part of the German Second Position atop a low but commanding ridge. From Pozières it was possible to look north-west to Thiepval. This area was still firmly in German hands, and as long as the Germans held Thiepval the British were going to find it very difficult to advance in the northern sector of the battlefield. With Pozières secured, the British could menace Thiepval from the rear. Moreover, a relatively modest advance from Pozières could make part of the German Second Line untenable, especially if High and Delville Woods also fell to Fourth Army, as seemed possible in the third week of July.

One of the reasons why 1st Australian Division's attack was successful is that the artillery support (which was mainly British) was highly effective, as was the performance of the Australian infantry. Also highly significant was the fact that the assault was well prepared by a competent and fairly experienced divisional staff, which had taken the trouble to consult with British divisions to glean their lessons of recent fighting. However, Gough had tried to pressurize Major General H.B. Walker, the British commander of the division, into attacking on 19 July, little more than a day after it had arrived on the Somme. What would probably have happened if Gough had had his way is shown by the fate of 2nd Australian Division, who relieved 1st Division in Pozières on the night of 25 July. The divisional commander, Major General J.G. Legge, was unable to stand up to Gough's urging and the Australians attacked on 29 July before preparations were fully complete, and he received little protection from his immediate superior, Lieutenant General W.R. Birdwood, I ANZAC Corps commander. The attack was a failure. A subsequent effort, on 4–5 August, was more successful; in all the two attacks cost the division 6,800 casualties.

Australian operations around Pozières were completed by 8 August. Casualties were heavy, not least because having captured German trenches the Australians were subjected to counter-attacks and, above all, to merciless shelling. 4th Pioneer Battalion of 2nd Division lost 220 men in ten days just trying to keep communication trenches in good repair. Pozières itself was smashed beyond recognition. One Australian soldier recalled that 'Gibraltar', a German strongpoint captured on 23 July, was the only intact edifice that rose from the ruins of the village.[13] A German attack in the early hours of 7 August against 4th Australian Division's positions to the north of Pozières was defeated, not least through the efforts of Lieutenant Albert Jacka, whose exploits on that day should have earned him a Bar to the VC he had won at Gallipoli.

CHAPTER 4

ATTRITION AND
ATTEMPTED BREAKTHROUGH
August to September 1916

Looking back at the Somme from a distance of nearly ninety years, the observer is struck by the failure of the British high command consistently to apply the methods of 14 July. When they did, the results could be spectacular. Delville Wood was subjected to a devastating bombardment on 27 July by the guns of XV and XIII Corps, 369 in all, exclusive of those used for counter-battery work. Such concentrated fire, targeted on a narrow frontage attacked by only two brigades, one each from 2nd and 5th Divisions, made the infantry's job relatively easy. The commander of 99 Brigade commented in an after-action report that although the fire of German infantry and machine-gunners was 'frequently very heavy' it was also 'extremely inaccurate (high), and this I attribute to the effect of our shell fire on the enemy's nerves'.[1] However, once the wood was captured the British infantry suffered heavily from German shelling and infantry counter-attacks.

By contrast, only two days later, 51st (Highland) Division made a fruitless attack – on a small scale, with the inadequate artillery support that was typical of this period of the battle – against High Wood. Guillemont was unsuccessfully attacked by 30th and 2nd Divisions on 30 July, and again by 2nd and 55th Divisions on 8 August. Both operations were marked by inadequate artillery support, very largely a consequence of the British gunners being assigned too many targets, thus reducing the intensity of the fire. On a small scale, it was 1 July all over again. Faulty methods were exacerbated by the new German tactic of thinning out their positions and holding shell holes, rather than lines of trenches which – as at Delville Wood on 27 July – were easily located by the Royal Artillery.[2] For the members of 55th Division in the trenches in front of Guillemont before the 8 August attack the 'bombardment was almost awe-inspiring in its intensity, and it might have been, with good reason, thought that nothing could live through it'.[3] They rapidly discovered that appearances could be dreadfully deceptive.

Perhaps 2 August 1916 marks the point at which Haig reluctantly accepted that the German Army on the Somme was not about to collapse. On the following day, the army commanders received instructions that admitted that the Germans had 'recovered to a great extent from the disorganisation' of early July. Their positions could not be attacked 'without careful and methodical preparation'.[4] Haig was undoubtedly right to reach this conclusion, that the battle was one of attrition, and not break-through. With this policy in mind, the fighting of the next six weeks becomes comprehensible. There were no assaults on the scale of 1 July. Instead, much of the fighting was designed to secure favourable positions for the next big attack, which was eventually to take place on 15 September. The rationale behind these 'line-straightening' operations was to make it as easy as possible for the artillery to do its job. At this stage of the war, the straighter the start line, the more likely it was that the artillery would be able to deliver shells accurately in support of the attacking infantry. In addition, experience had shown that as far as infantry attacks were concerned, the simpler the plan the better; and a meandering jumping-off point could prove a dangerous complication. But, as Peter Simkins has noted, 'the broader tactical benefits were not always instantly apparent to the officers and men who saw the strength of their battalions progressively eroded by minor yet costly "line-straightening" operations.'[5]

However, Haig's demand for painstaking preparation before attacks, to be clear 'that everything possible has been done to ensure success', was more honoured in the breach than the observance. While the defence of inexperience on the part of commanders, staff officers and troops cannot be entirely discounted, the hard fact remains that too often a boy was sent to do a man's job. A year later, during Plumer's operations at Third Ypres, the BEF carried out larger scale 'joined-up' attacks, but this was a period in which artillery skills had improved considerably. Line-straightening was important, but the piecemeal way in which it was carried out on the Somme was a waste of resources and, more importantly, lives. In late August Haig wrote to Rawlinson in terms that could have left him in little doubt that the C-in-C was unhappy with Fourth Army's repeated attacks with inadequate forces on narrow fronts.

The beginning of August gave some more illustrations of the problems of conducting coalition warfare. Haig and Foch agreed that the French and British would co-operate in an attack in the Guillemont area on 7 August, with both armies joining together in a subsequent operation on a front from the Somme river to Maurepas and Falfemont Farm on 11 August. In the event, the British had to postpone their attack until 8 August, with results we have already noted, while the French went ahead as planned. The Franco-British attack planned for 11 August was postponed until the following day. The British part consisted of a mere two companies of a battalion of 55th Division, which made some gains near Guillemont, but were withdrawn because the left-hand French unit was held up. Further south, the French did much better. Fayolle's Sixth Army seized much of the German Second Position on a front of some 2 1/2 miles from Maurepas to Clery.

On 11 August Joffre gave vent to his unhappiness with the progress of the battle and, more particularly, Haig's conduct of it. He wanted to move away from the small-scale battles, replacing them instead by broad-front multi-divisional affairs, involving both British and French forces, and outlined some ambitious proposals. In the event, the two men agreed on a combined attack on

18 August in the Guillemont-Maurepas area. The weather broke on 14 August, bringing heavy rain, and therefore mud, adding another layer of friction to the activities of the troops. Unfortunately, a preliminary operation on 16 August was checked. This had an adverse effect on the attack that began two days later. On 18 August British XIV, XV and III Corps attacked alongside the French. The Allies inched forward, but at heavy cost. 3rd Rifle Brigade, a battalion of 24th Division, crossed no man's land without suffering heavy losses, 'leaning' on the barrage, and then came up against German troops described as 'determined and courageous'. The result of this 'fierce fight' was the capture of about 100 unwounded prisoners, who were set to work to put the captured position into a state of defence. Later, Guillemont Station was taken, but Guillemont village proved beyond the attackers. When 3rd Rifle Brigade attacked the village on 21 August, they were unable to capitalize on this earlier success: 'the village of Guillemont was held in great force with strong supports in tunnel dugouts. No sooner were front line troops shot down than they were replaced from the supports.'[6] The attack was a failure, and Guillemont remained in German hands.

A further combined British-French offensive was delayed until 3 September, and the remainder of August saw the by now familiar mix of narrow-front, sporadic attacks. These did bring some successes. On 24 August 14th (Light) Division (XV Corps) began an operation to clear Delville Wood. On their flank, 33rd Division's attack between High and Delville Woods was supported by tactical innovation in the shape of a machine-gun barrage. 100th Machine Gun Company, using ten guns, fired a twelve-hour continuous barrage in support of the infantry. Nearly 1 million rounds were expended, one gun team alone firing 120,000 rounds. Not surprisingly, by the end of this marathon 'many of the NCOs and gunners were almost asleep on their feet from sheer exhaustion', but the barrage materially assisted 33rd Division's success.[7]

RESERVE ARMY OPERATIONS IN AUGUST

In Reserve Army's sector, Gough's command also fought a series of grinding, attritional actions during August. The Australian actions around Pozières were succeeded by attacks at roughly right angles to the Bapaume road, towards Mouquet Farm, which was half-way between Pozières and Thiepval. Gains in this area offered the enticing prospect of taking the fortress of Thiepval from the rear. From 9 August to 3 September, three Australian divisions (4th, 1st and 2nd) carried out seven separate attacks towards 'Moo Cow Farm' (this was the Australian version: the British called it 'Mucky Farm'). Invariably conducted on a narrow front, this allowed the Germans to bring heavy firepower to bear on the attackers. In all, the Australians suffered 23,000 casualties in six weeks. They had lost about the same number of men in eight months at Gallipoli, the year before.

The Australians were not, of course, the only formations to be committed to narrow-front, 'battering ram' attacks by Gough. II Corps (Lieutenant General Sir Claud Jacob) fought alongside the Anzacs, and 12th, 48th and 49th Divisions were all engaged during August in some small-scale operations that none the less took their toll in casualties. In the middle of the month, 25th Division came into action. From 23 July this division had been conducting trench warfare north of the Ancre, firing its artillery and machine-guns in support of offensive operations in the southern part of Reserve Army's sector.

On 18 August, the day of the big combined attack by the French and Fourth Army, Gough, under orders from Haig, had also committed his troops to battle. 48th Division, aided by a smoke discharge from opposite Thiepval and effective artillery fire, captured some ground around the Nab, although 1st Australian Division on their flank had less success. The operations of 48th and 25th Divisions between 21 and 27 August brought Leipzig Salient under British control. But Thiepval, the key bastion of the German defences in the northern part of the battlefield, remained frustratingly beyond Reserve Army's grasp.

Verey lights (flares) at night, Thiepval, 7 August 1916. There was much activity in no man's land at night, as both sides sent out patrols and repaired wire defences.

Gough's next move coincided with the Franco-British offensive south of the Bapaume road. On 3 September he used one division (39th) to assault north of the Ancre, and 49th Division to the south, opposite Thiepval. 25th Division (II Corps) attacked the Wonder Work, and 4th Australian Division (I ANZAC Corps), advanced against Fabeck Graben. The Australians had some success but elsewhere the offensive was a failure. Despite some careful preparations for the attack, including laying out tapes during the previous night, and considerable determination on the part of the troops, 25th Division failed to take the position and fell back to their own trenches. The divisional history records that 'Casualties were very heavy indeed'; two battalion commanders were killed, and 'Large numbers of wounded remained out in No Man's Land throughout the day'.[8] 25th Division attacked on a frontage of only 500 yards, which was further testimony to the problems of assaulting on such a narrow front. Reserve Army's major success in this period was 11th Division's capture of the Wonder Work on 14

September, the very eve of Haig's next 'big push'.

On Fourth Army's front, there was more success. 20th (Light) Division prised the defenders out of Guillemont on 3 September, and on their right flank 5th Division made a substantial advance into the German Second Position. By the early hours of 5 September it had captured Falfemont Farm, and then pushed forward into Leuze Wood. An attack on Ginchy by 7th Division was, however, unsuccessful. Fighting also raged in the area of Delville and High Woods – timely reminders that the business begun in mid July was still not finished. Lieutenant Ernst Jünger of 73rd Hanoverian Fusiliers fought at Guillemont, and he left a graphic account of what it was like to be on the receiving end of a British attack at this time, as clumsy as it might be. He stressed the extent to which the defenders felt themselves to be outgunned by the British, and highly vulnerable to shellfire. He complained that while German artillery observation balloons were conspicuous by their absence, 'on the English side there were thirty at once over one spot, observing every movement with argus eyes and at once directing a hail of iron upon it'. Jünger was to live to write books that revealed a fascination with the brutality of modern war. 'It was the days at Guillemont,' he was later to write, 'that first made me aware of the overwhelming effects of the war of material. We had to adapt ourselves to an entirely new phase of war,' one dominated by artillery fire. German losses were magnified by the 'old Prussian obstinacy' of holding ground for its own sake, and crowding troops into the front lines. As he looked around the moonscape produced by high explosive and shrapnel, Jünger was struck by the irony that such scenes were produced 'by men who intended them to be a decisive end to the war'.[9]

Ginchy fell to Major General W.B. Hickie's 16th (Irish) Division on 9 September. The contribution to the British Empire's war effort made by the constitutional Nationalist community in Ireland has been largely neglected, but this formation was the Catholic and Nationalist counterpart of the Protestant and Unionist 36th (Ulster) Division. Of the two brigades committed on 9 September, 47 Brigade lost heavily to shelling, and made little progress. The

Thiepval

Mouquet

Zig Zag Trench

Q

Wonder
Work

Hohenzollern Trench

Ulmer Graben

Constance Trench

Pole Trench

Skyline Trench

Hindenburg Trench

N a b   V a l l e y

Leipzig
Salient

Ration Trench

XXX
II

The Nab

Fourth

Nordwerk

Tr.

Ration

Authuille
Wood

THE RESERVE ARMY FRONT,
AUGUST 1916

German Front Line, 1st August

Ground gained 1st to 5th Augu:

Ground gained 6th to 19th Aug

Ground gained 20th to 31st Au

Trench

Land over 140m
120 – 140m
100 – 120m
Land under 100m

Zollern   Graben   Courcelette

0.6.2.

Fabeck   Graben

Graben   0.6.I.

Trench   Bapaume 5m

Park   Lane   0. 6. 2.
                      The Elbow
                      0. 6. I.

Western   Cemetery   Mill

                              0.6.2
                              0.6.I.

                                        Torr Trench Munster Alley

Trench   N

Pozières

Albert 3.5m   xxx   xxxx
                   I ANZAC   Fourth

0   500   1000   1500
                Yards

British infantry moving up in support over a devastated landscape near Ginchy, September 1916.

brigade commander succinctly recorded the reasons for failure as 'enemy's trenches were untouched by our artillery, their morale was unshaken and, when we attacked, we found them fully prepared'. In these circumstances, no troops could hope to succeed. On the flank, 48 Brigade was more successful, pushing on into Ginchy, overcoming the defenders but suffering heavy casualties. A recent study has concluded that 16th Division 'fought well on the Somme', and the capture of Ginchy certainly offers support for this view.[10]

The French were not inactive in this period. On 3 September Fayolle's Sixth Army pushed forward strongly on Rawlinson's flank, and when Falfemont Farm fell, the two armies were able to make contact across the Combles Ravine. Micheler's Tenth Army attacked on 4 September at the extreme south of the Allied line, and found themselves in an indecisive fight. Friedrich Steinbrecher, a young German officer, wrote his impressions of this fighting. He wrote of being rushed up to oppose a French attack in the Chaulnes/Vermandovillers area, and being thrown into the counter-attack against a breakthrough:

> We advanced through a shattered wood in a hail of shells. I don't know how I found the right way. Then across an expanse of shell-craters, on and on. Falling down and getting up again. Machine guns were firing. I had to cut across our own barrage and the enemy's. I am untouched. At last we reach the front line. Frenchmen are forcing their way in. The tide of battle ebbs and flows... Day melts into night. We are always on the alert... Somme. The whole history of the world cannot contain a more ghastly word![11]

By 15 September the British had forced themselves forward on to a reasonable jumping-off position for a major attack. The line was not perfect. Despite the efforts of XIV Corps, the Quadrilateral, a formidable strongpoint that blocked an advance east from the Delville/Ginchy area, remained in German possession. This, and the fact Reserve Army had yet to capture Fabeck Graben, was a sobering indication of how little territory the BEF had captured in two and a half months of what the British official historian referred to as a 'slow and costly advance' on the Somme.[12] True, the Germans had also suffered grievously, and in those weeks British troops and commanders had gained invaluable experience; but it was a terrible price to pay for meagre tangible gains.

GERMANY: CHANGES AT THE TOP

By the end of August 1916 Falkenhayn's strategy lay in ruins. The Verdun offensive was going nowhere, the Central Powers were still under pressure from the Russians in the East, and while the Allies had failed to break through on the Somme, the Germans were still being forced back. Perhaps the final straw was the entry of Romania into the war on the side of the *entente* powers on 27 August. In fact by the end of 1916 Romania was defeated by a hastily deployed German force, but the appearance of yet another enemy at a time when the Central Powers were under severe pressure did little to staunch the haemorrhaging of Falkenhayn's support among the German élite. He was removed from his position on 29 August.

Falkenhayn was replaced as Chief of the General Staff by General Paul von Hindenburg. General Erich Ludendorff was made First Quartermaster General, in effect Hindenburg's deputy, although in many ways Ludendorff was the dominant figure in the partnership. Hindenburg and Ludendorff had made their reputations on the Eastern Front, and came westward to pick up the burden of defence in the West. The two new generals had immense power. By the end of 1916, they had effectively established a military dictatorship in Germany, pushing the kaiser to the margins of decision-making.

Falkenhayn commented that 'it was only with great anxiety that he contemplated the certainty that a change of Chief [of the General Staff], under the circumstances, must inevitably mean a change of system in the conduct of the war'.[13] Hindenburg and Ludendorff were total warriors. The Somme demonstrated

Field Marshal Paul von Hindenburg. Kitchener was Hindenburg's nearest equivalent in Britain. Both men became symbols of their respective national war efforts.

Britain's willingness and ability to transform economic power into military might, and they believed that Germany could only prevail against the *entente* by moving towards an all-out conflict. The 'Hindenburg Programme' mobilized Germany's economy and population for total war. This of course was the very path that Falkenhayn had rejected, concluding that the Central Powers were unlikely to win against the greater resources of the *entente*. In the long term, the effects of this radical, hastily implemented and wildly over-ambitious plan were disastrous for the German war effort. As one historian has written: 'In his pursuit of an ill-conceived total mobilization for the attainment of irrational goals, Ludendorff undermined the strength of the army, promoted economic instability, created administrative chaos, and set loose an orgy of interest politics.'[14] All this was, in time, to have serious consequences for the willingness of the German population to make sacrifices for the Hohenzollern regime, which was a significant factor in the collapse of Germany in 1918. This was a direct effect of the battle of the Somme.

The reshuffling of the German command team also had an influence on the battlefield. Crown Prince Rupprecht of Bavaria took command of a 'Group of Armies' encompassing First, Second, Sixth and Seventh Armies. The Imperial Crown Prince, the Kaiser's son Wilhelm, assumed command of a second Group of Armies that absorbed all but one of the remaining formations. Moreover, shortly after taking over command, Hindenburg issued a new regulation for 'The Defensive Battle'. This was a move away from the idea of holding the front line at all costs and immediately counterattacking every enemy lodgement. Rather:

> The object of battle defence consists in letting the attacker wear himself out, bleeding himself white, but saving our own forces. The defence will be conducted not by putting in line large numbers of men, but mainly by inserting machines (artillery, minenwerfers, machine guns etc)… In the distribution of forces, the fundamental consideration is the saving of personnel.[15]

These new instructions gave official approval to what was already happening on the battlefield. Effectively, this move towards defence in depth, or 'elastic' defence, marked an important point in the emergence of modern defensive tactics. OHL took it a stage further than the rudimentary version occurring on the Somme by ordering the building of the Siegfried Stellung or, as the British called it, the Hindenburg Line, some 15–20 miles to the rear. Work

Above: General Erich Ludendorff. Hindenburg's partnership with Ludendorff was initially remarkably successful but ultimately led Germany to disaster.

on this dense belt of defences based around concrete 'pillbox' fortifications began on 23 September. It was to be the focus of heavy fighting in 1917 and 1918.

FLERS-COURCELETTE

The battle of Flers–Courcelette, which began on 15 September 1916, is today remembered mainly for the debut of the tank, a new type of weapon that would eventually transform the face of the battlefield. Haig, the supposed technophobe, actually had high expectations of this new and unproven piece of technology, just as he had of gas before the battle of Loos the previous September. In mid August 1916 he had written of tanks: 'I hope and think that they will add very greatly to the prospects of success and to the extent of it.'[16] In many ways, the tank was an obvious product of trench warfare: a vehicle with tracks that could cope with the difficult terrain, and armour which afforded the crew a measure of protection. It is important to be aware of what the tank was capable of doing in September 1916. It could crush barbed wire and bring up fire support close to the infantry, and it was effective, at least initially, as a psychological weapon, scaring enemy troops and boosting the morale of friendly soldiers. It was nowhere nearly as effective as its distant relations of the Second World War, which had undergone twenty years more of technological development. In 1916 it was slow, capable of moving at only about 2 mph, and it was mechanically unreliable. Moreover, for tank crews operations were ordeals composed of extreme heat and breathing in carbon monoxide. The tank was quite incapable of long-distance pursuit. On all these counts the tank of 1916 vintage was not a battle-winning weapon, although the improved models that appeared in 1917 and 1918 slotted into a battle-winning weapons *system*. Critics such as Lloyd George, who subsequently attacked Haig for revealing the secret of the tank before large numbers became available, displayed a tenuous grip on the realities of the Western Front in September 1916. For the BEF, fighting as the junior coalition partner in a

Materielschlacht, the battle had to be a case of 'maximum effort'. If Haig had been right to use the tanks on 15 September, two other decisions deserve further scrutiny. First, was it right for Rawlinson to 'penny-packet' the tanks, or should they have been massed in one punch? Of forty-eight tanks that were 'runners' on 15 September, only about twenty-one actually got into action. Using the tanks in small numbers as a kind of mobile pillbox to bring fire support to the infantry was as good a way as any of using them, bearing in mind their technological limitations. Second, Rawlinson decided to leave gaps in the barrage, to avoid churning up the ground over which the tanks would have to advance. While possibly sensible in theory, in practice it meant that parts of the German line were untouched by shelling, the very thing that was able to suppress enemy resistance. This mistake was magnified by the fact that the tanks were assigned defensive strongpoints to attack. This tactical error was to have harsh consequences on 15 September.[17]

The battle of Flers–Courcelette was a multi-divisional push on a frontage that stretched from Reserve Army's sector, right across Fourth Army's front; French Sixth Army also attacked on 15 September, although at a later time than the British. Haig set ambitious objectives for this offensive. This was, like 1 July, an attempt to reopen mobile operations; once again, he believed that German morale was on the verge of cracking. A gap was to be punched in the German Third Position between Flers and Courcelette, the latter village to be captured by the Canadians of Reserve Army. Then the Cavalry Corps, with two divisions in the lead, was to leapfrog through the assault troops and seize Bapaume as the first stage in rolling up the German defences. Rawlinson, as on 1 July, preferred a more limited effort to capture the German positions, using a step by step approach. Haig thought Rawlinson's approach to be too cautious, and imposed his will on the Fourth Army commander.

In the run-up to the battle, the Royal Artillery fired 828,000 shells. The bombardment was of an intensity that was better than that of 1 July, 'but less than half' the intensity of the shelling

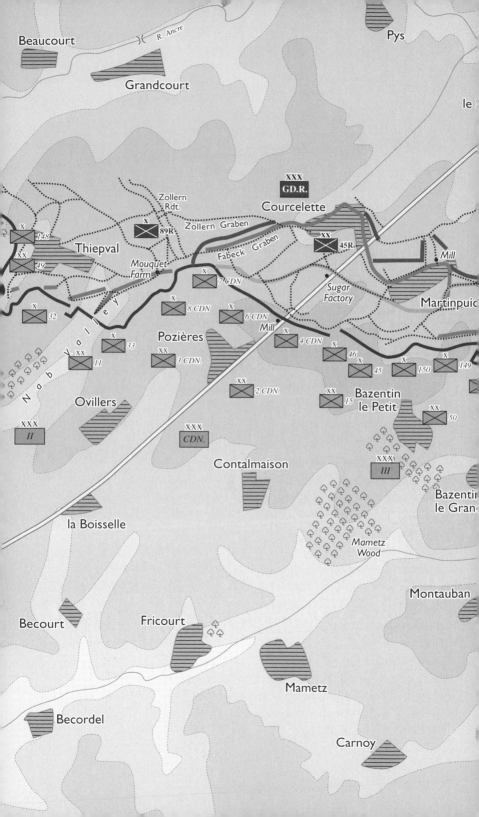

Beaucourt

R. Ancre

Pys

Grandcourt

XXX
GD.R.

Courcelette

Zollern
Rdt.

X 89R
Zollern Graben

X 148
Thiepval
XX 49
Mouquet
Farm
Fabeck Graben

XX 45R.

Martinpuic

Sugar
Factory

Mill

X 7 CDN

X 32

X 8 CDN

X 6 CDN
Mill

X 33
Pozières
XX 11
X 3 CDN.

X 4 CDN

X 46
X 45

X 150

X 149

Ovillers

XX 2 CDN.

XX 15
Bazentin
le Petit

XX 50

XXX
II

XXX
CDN.

Contalmaison

XXX
III

Bazenti
le Gran

la Boisselle

Mametz
Wood

Montauban

Becourt

Fricourt

Mametz

Becordel

Carnoy

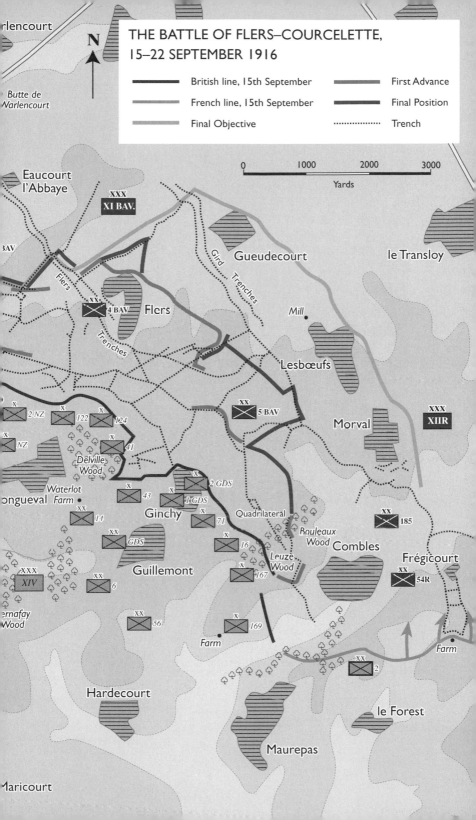

THE BATTLE OF FLERS–COURCELETTE,
15–22 SEPTEMBER 1916

British line, 15th September	First Advance
French line, 15th September	Final Position
Final Objective	Trench

0   1000   2000   3000
Yards

N

rlencourt

Butte de
Warlencourt

Eaucourt
l'Abbaye

XXX
XI BAV.

BAV

Flers

Gueudecourt

le Transloy

XX
4 BAV

Flers

Gird
Trenches

Mill

Trenches

Lesbœufs

X
2 NZ

X
122

X
124

XX
5 BAV

Morval

XXX
XIIR

X
NZ

X
41

Délville
Wood

X
2 GDS

X
43

X
1 GDS

Ginchy

X
71

Quadrilateral

Rouleaux
Wood

Combles

XX
185

Frégicourt

XX
14

XX
GDS

Guillemont

X
16

Leuze
Wood

XX
54R

Waterlot Farm

ongueval

XXX
XIV

XX
6

X
167

XX
56

X
169

Farm

XX
2

Farm

ernafay
Wood

Hardecourt

le Forest

Maurepas

Maricourt

British gunners posing with heavy shells. Captain Fryatt was a merchant skipper captured and executed by the Germans for trying to ram a U-boat menacing his vessel.

employed for the successful attack of 14 July.[18] This failure to provide the requisite weight of shells was to be a significant factor in the disappointing outcome of the battle.

On the front of XIV Corps, the right-hand British formation, 56th Division made little progress against strong German defences with uncut wire; the same fate befell 6th Division on their left. The Quadrilateral, a major German strongpoint, was located in a tank lane. Thus the machine-guns situated in this position were not suppressed by artillery, and were able to bring heavy fire to bear on the flanks of 56th and Guards Divisions, and caused heavy casualties among the troops of 6th Division advancing to the front of the Quadrilateral. Of the fifteen tanks that were supposed to attack this position and two others, Bouleaux Wood and the Triangle, only two actually took part in the fighting.

Of the three divisions of XIV Corps, the left-hand formation, Guards Division, advancing out of Ginchy, achieved the most. Its objective was the village of Lesboeufs, some 3,000 yards distant. 1st Guards Brigade, on the right of the division, was held up by heavy fire from Pint Trench; Lieutenant Colonel J.V. Campbell of 3rd Coldstream Guards rallied the confused mass of Guardsmen from various units with the aid of a hunting horn and led them to the next objective, winning the VC in the process. The tanks allocated to the Guards Division 'proved of little or no assistance to the infantry', having lagged behind or 'lost all sense of direction and wandered about aimlessly'.[19] The Guards advanced about half-way to their final objective on 15 September.

14th (Light) Division, on the left of the Guards Division, made some progress. 42 Brigade advanced to just short of Bulls Road, which ran between Flers and Lesboeufs, creating a salient whose flanks were subject to machine-gun fire. The neighbouring formation, Major General S.T.B. Lawford's 41st Division, was the junior division of the New Army and had only been in France for a few months. It carried out the most famous advance of the day, capturing the village of Flers. An RFC observer reported watching

the infantry move over the open behind the barrage which crept ahead with uncanny precision. He saw a continuous stream of emergency signals bursting above the German trenches. Within ten minutes of the British infantry starting forward their flares were being lit along the Switch Line [41st Division's first objective]... So rapidly indeed had the infantry moved that they had outdistanced their supporting tanks. At half-past eight, however, three tanks were seen moving towards Flers, and fifteen minutes later one of them was advancing down the main street surrounded by a crowd of khaki figures, who were soon afterwards seen to occupy the north and west of the village.[20]

The tank was D-17, commanded by Lieutenant S.H. Hastie. This report was immortalized by a highly coloured version that

New Zealand medical personnel, wearing their distinctive 'lemon squeezer' hats. The New Zealand Division was to earn an impressive reputation on the battlefield.

appeared in the press: 'A tank is walking up the High Street of Flers with the British Army cheering behind.'[21]

Attacking between Delville and High Woods was the New Zealand Division. This was the first major action of the 'Kiwis' on the Western Front, although they had previously earned a reputation in Gallipoli as good fighting troops. They rapidly captured the Switch Line, which is where the New Zealand memorial is situated today. The New Zealanders betrayed some of their inexperience by twice advancing into the British barrage. The progress of the 47th Division on their left flank was somewhat slower, with the inevitable consequence of German machine-guns from High Wood catching the New Zealanders in enfilade.

> While some of the occupants [of Switch Trench] made a poor fight [the divisional historian recorded], others, stouter hearted, threw bombs and fired rifles till our lines were atop of them, and then on the greater part of the front, throwing down their weapons, they held up their hands, and with calculated presumption called for mercy. Mercy, however, was shown only to the Red Cross men and the wounded. Where further resistance was made, the enemy in the trench itself were disposed of after a little point-blank shooting and a short struggle with bombs.[22]

While this divisional history was more candid than most, one should envisage similar activities occurring along the whole front. By the end of the day, with the aid of two tanks that arrived belatedly, the New Zealand Division had linked up with 41st Division in the area of Flers. The three divisions of Horne's XV Corps, 14th, 41st and New Zealand, did well on 15 September; but their advance fell short of expectation.

One of the toughest jobs of 15 September fell to 47th (London) Division, which was ordered to capture High Wood. Believing that the front lines were too close to allow a bombardment, Lieutenant General Pulteney, the commander of III Corps, decided to use tanks as a substitute for artillery in High Wood. A sensible alternative would have been for the British troops to evacuate their front-line trenches just before the bombardment. Two months of fighting had reduced the wood to a landscape of shell holes and shattered stumps. It was extremely unpromising terrain in which to commit the fragile tank of 1916 vintage. In spite of warnings emanating from the tank crews themselves, relayed via Major General Barter, Pulteney insisted that the tanks be launched into High Wood. In the event, only one tank, D-13, succeeded in getting any distance into the wood, and its support to the infantry, while useful, was scarcely decisive. With the aid of a hurricane trench mortar barrage that hurled 750 Stokes mortar bombs in the space of fifteen minutes, and with neighbouring divisions outflanking the German defenders, the London Territorial infantry finally captured High Wood – an objective that, of course, should have been secured on 14 July or even on the first day of the Somme offensive. The capture of High Wood was a significant achievement, but it was merely 47th Division's first objective on 15 September, and the division could not get any further forward, leaving the New Zealand Division on its right holding a pronounced salient. Barter unfairly paid the price of his division's relative lack of success. Pulteney, who was himself culpable, relieved Barter of his command on the grounds of his 'wanton waste of men'.[23]

Another territorial division, 50th (Northumbrian), on the left of 47th, committed two brigades to the assault. Although hampered by enfilade fire from High Wood, the division made some ground, particularly on its right, where it linked up with the neighbouring division in the Martinpuich area. This village fell to the 15th (Scottish) Division. An effective bombardment eased the task for the infantry, although there were some pockets of German resistance. The capture of Martinpuich meant that a key part of the German defences had passed into British hands.

Two divisions of Reserve Army also went into action on 15 September. On that day, the Canadian Corps made their Somme debut, attacking astride the Albert–Bapaume road. In bitter fighting, Major General R.E.W. Turner's 2nd Canadian Division seized the village of Courcelette. As in many other places that day, the tanks were unable to keep up with the pace of the infantry, but they had some limited impact. One tank, C-5, nicknamed 'Crème de

Menthe', took part in the capture of the sugar factory on the outskirts of Courcelette, firing its 6-pounder guns against machine-gun posts. A report of 4th Canadian Brigade asserted that 'The tanks, used for the first time, proved their value,'[24] although here as elsewhere, the artillery/infantry combination was the battle winner. The actions of Major General L.J. Lipsett's 3rd Canadian Division, on the flank of Turner's 2nd, marked the extreme left of the Allied assault on 15 September. They took some important sections of the Fabeck Graben.

Karl Gorzel, a German soldier, left an account of the fighting at Thiepval at this time. Under a heavy bombardment:

> Hour after hour passed... The fire increases to such bewildering intensity that it is no longer possible to distinguish between the crashes. Our mouths and ears are full of earth; three times bruised and three times dug up again, we wait – wait for night or the enemy!...
>
> Suddenly the barrage lifts – the shells are falling behind us – and there, close in front, is the first wave of the enemy! Release at last! Everyone who is not wounded, everyone who can raise an arm, is up, and like a shower of hailstones our bombs pelt upon the attacking foe! The first wave lies prone in front of our holes, and already the second is upon us, and behind the English are coming on in a dense mass. Anyone who reaches our line is at once polished off in a hand to hand bayonet fight...[25]

The sober conclusion of the British official historian on 15 September was that the German Army had 'been dealt a severe blow', but that Fourth Army's accomplishments 'fell far short of the desired achievement'. This assessment is fair. The German line had sagged under the onslaught, but had not entirely given way. The British had taken the German Third Position on a front of 4,500 yards, and advanced 2,500 yards – 1,000 yards further than in the Flers area. The territory gained 'was about twice that gained

A Royal Fusilier of Major General Maxse's 18th (Eastern) Division with 'souvenirs' captured in Thiepval, 26-27 September 1916.

on 1 July and at about half the cost in casualties'.[26] Yet Fourth Army had been unable to take immediate advantage of these gains. The defenders had rushed up reinforcements to counter the threat of a breakthrough in the Flers sector. But the casualties, exhaustion and disorganization even of successful troops – as with 41st Division – militated against such a breakthrough. Neither was there, as on 1 July, the partial compensation of substantial French success south of the River Somme; on the right flank, four French corps attacked on 15 September, without achieving much progress. By the standards of 1916, the battle of Flers–Courcelette was a moderately successful set-piece battle. It placed the BEF in a good position to renew the offensive against the German Third Position. Haig's plan had been over-ambitious; and given the mistakes in the use of artillery and tanks, and the general low level of experience in the BEF at that time, it would have been surprising if his divisions had achieved anything more on 15 September. For the second time, Haig had planned for a substantial breakthrough on the Somme and for the second time it had failed to materialize.

Perhaps the last word on Flers–Courcelette can be left to the Rev. W.E. Drury, a chaplain attached to 56th (London) Division:

> The glory and success of September 15th I did not see, but the cost of it I shall never forget… Whereas [at the Main Dressing Station] on ordinary days one triple tent for officers and one for men sufficed, now all the rows of them were in use and the ground outside was covered in stretchers. This was in spite of the fact that the walking wounded did not come our way. It must be remembered, too, that ours was only one of a number of main Dressing Stations receiving the streams of wounded that flowed down from behind the attack. Just as Regimental Aid Posts fed Advanced Dressing Stations from various points on the battlefield, and just as several Advanced Stations combined to fill our camp, so we united with others to replenish one of the Casualty Clearing Stations which linked those sectors engaged in the attack… In time the tide of wounded coming down from the battlefield of September 15th began to ebb and we were reduced again to the ordinary influx of maimed men.[27]

CHAPTER 5

MORVAL TO THE ANCRE

THE AIR BATTLE: ANOTHER SWING OF THE PENDULUM

From mid September, the German air service began to mount a serious challenge to the Allies' control of the skies. New aircraft, the Fokker D II, Halberstadt D II and the Albatros D I and D III, replaced the Fokker E I and proved superior to their British opponents. They were organized into new units, *Jagdstaffeln* or 'hunting squadrons', manned by experienced pilots. *Jagdstaffel Jasta 2*, commanded by the ace pilot Oswald Boelcke was sent to the Somme. His pilots included Manfred von Richthofen. An air battle on 17 September between a patrol led by Boelcke of *Jasta 2* and BE2 Cs and FE 2Bs signalled the end of Allied domination. The Albatros demonstrated its superiority over British aircraft, and von Richthofen claimed his first two victims.[1]

Gwilym Lewis, an RFC scout pilot, noted on 23 October that the nature of the air campaign was beginning to change:

> just at present we are living in busy times. The Huns are making the best effort to take over the air supremacy they have made since July, and a lively time they are giving we poor wretched DH pilots who are responsible for keeping them back… the good days of July and August, when two or three DHs used to push half-a-dozen Huns onto the chimney tops of Bapaume, are no more.[2]

During the latter part of the Somme the RFC was at a disadvantage, but the Germans did not succeed in establishing a degree of control of the air comparable to that which the British enjoyed until mid September. However by the end of the month, over much of French Sixth Army's sector, 'the Germans enjoyed unchallenged air supremacy', despite being at a three to one numerical disadvantage.[3] The Germans were to expand this ascendancy during 1917. With good reason, the RFC was to remember the month in which the battle of Arras was launched as 'bloody April'.

THE FOURTH ARMY AT MORVAL

Just ten days after the disappointment of the attack of 15 September, Fourth Army's efforts were rewarded by success in the battle of Morval. Given the opportunity to co-operate with the French, GHQ had decided to postpone a fresh major attack until 21 September, and therefore to attack, as the French desired, in the middle of the day. A number of limited attacks were mounted to secure a good jumping-off line for this attack; thus the Quadrilateral was taken by 6th Division on 18 September. Lacking darkness to cover the approach of the tanks to the front line during the forthcoming attack, Rawlinson decreed that tanks were to be placed in reserve, so the creeping barrage would be continuous across the front to be attacked. This fortuitous decision greatly facilitated the attack, which was delayed by poor weather conditions until 25 September, as did the fact that the objectives were significantly weaker than the positions attacked ten days earlier. The British were to assault only one German trench system; as a preliminary, the artillery fired a bombardment some '40 per cent heavier' than that of 15 September.[4] This combination of a more intense bombardment and weaker defensive positions opened the way for successful infantry attacks across the entire front.

The attack began at 12.35 p.m. Following a creeping barrage, the infantry of XIV Corps (56th, 5th, 6th, and Guards Divisions) rapidly overran the German trenches. Although the battle was effectively decided by firepower, in the midst of industrialized warfare several individuals demonstrated the continuing importance of leadership. Lieutenant Colonel P.V.P. Stone, personally leading 1st Norfolks, 'treated the attack as a pheasant shoot, with his servant as loader'. In the same brigade of 5th Division, Private 'Todger' Jones, of 1st Cheshires, won the VC for capturing 100 Germans and bringing them back to the British lines. 5th Division captured Morval, while Lesboeufs fell to 6th and Guards Divisions. One Grenadier described this attack as 'one of the most successful operations in which the Guards Division was engaged... The preparation seems to have been complete, and every possible contingency foreseen.'[5]

XV Corps (21st, 55th, New Zealand Divisions) was nearly as successful. On 55th Division's front:

> the infantry kept closer to the barrage than ever before, preferring to suffer some casualties from possible short shells from their own gunners, rather than to run the risk of allowing the barrage to get away from them and of being compelled to face the enemy's uninterrupted machine gun and rifle fire, as had on more than one occasion happened previously. The result was eminently successful. Thanks to the excellence of the barrage and to the splendid dash of the infantry in keeping up to it, the enemy was unable to bring his machine guns into action in time, and the whole of the first objective was captured with few casualties.[6]

This combination of a tactical learning curve with success at the operational level epitomizes the reasons for the success of Fourth Army at the battle of Morval. Interestingly, tanks played no part in the successes of 25 September.

Gueudecourt was supposed to be taken by 21st Division, but proved to be too tough a nut to crack on 25 September. It fell to a dismounted cavalry patrol on the following day, having been abandoned by the Germans. Similarly, Combles fell on 26th September, the London Scottish meeting up with French troops in the town following the German withdrawal. Otherwise, the gains of French Sixth Army in the battle of Morval had been disappointingly meagre.

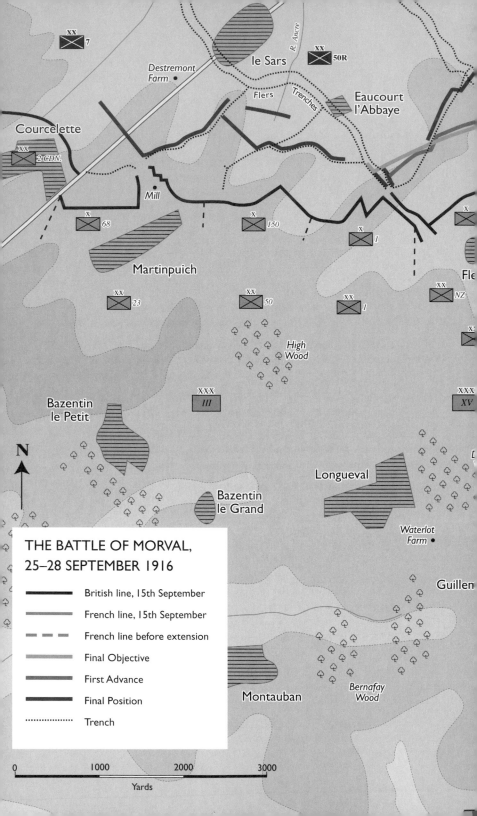

THE BATTLE OF MORVAL,
25–28 SEPTEMBER 1916

British line, 15th September
French line, 15th September
French line before extension
Final Objective
First Advance
Final Position
Trench

0   1000   2000   3000

Yards

le Sars
Destremont Farm
Flers
Trenches
Eaucourt l'Abbaye
Courcelette
Mill
Martinpuich
High Wood
Bazentin le Petit
Bazentin le Grand
Longueval
Waterlot Farm
Guillen
Montauban
Bernafay Wood
R. Ancre
Fle
N

Beaulencourt

le Transloy

6 BAV. XX

Gueudecourt

Gird Trenches

Mill

55

X *110*

X *64*

X *3 GDS*

Lesbœufs

XX *52R*

XXX **XXVIR**

X *1 GDS*

XX *GDS*

X *18*

X *16*

Morval

XX *6*

X *15*

XX *5*

X *95*

XX *168*

Ginchy

Bouleaux Wood

Combles

XX *56*

X *167*

Leuze Wood

XX *51R*

Frégicourt

X *169*

Farm

Farm

Maurepas

XXXX Sixth

RESERVE ARMY: THE BATTLES OF THIEPVAL RIDGE AND ANCRE HEIGHTS, SEPTEMBER – NOVEMBER 1916

Morval was not the only good news to reach GHQ at this time. On Reserve Army's front, two key and much contested positions finally fell into British hands. When Gough began the battle of Thiepval Ridge on 26 September, it represented the largest scale operation yet attempted by Reserve Army. On the right of the line, 2nd and 1st Canadian Divisions advanced about 1,000 yards to the north of Courcelette, while 11th Division seized Mouquet Farm. To the last, German resistance was stiff around this area. Three battalions of 11th Division in particular, 5th Dorsets, 8th Northumberland Fusiliers, and 9th Lancashire Fusiliers suffered grievously in the fighting.

The jewel in Reserve Army's crown was undoubtedly the capture of Thiepval. Maxse's 18th (Eastern) Division had already acquired a reputation for competence as a result of its exploits on 1 July and at the taking of Trônes Wood a fortnight later. Maxse believed that 'With sufficient time to prepare an assault on a definite and limited objective, I believe that a well trained division can capture almost any "impregnable" stronghold, and this doctrine has been taught to the 18th Division.'[7] Certainly, the capture of Thiepval had the divisional hallmark of careful preparation and training. According to an officer of 54th Brigade: 'everyone was full of confidence. The troops were trained to the minute; attack formations had been practised till it could be expected that the advance would push through to its final objective as a drill movement, whatever the obstacles or casualties. It was known, too, that the artillery preparation had been terrific.'[8] The battle was by no means a walk-over, and neither did it go entirely to order. The Schwaben Redoubt as well as Thiepval was supposed to fall on 26 September, but this plan proved to be too ambitious. Thiepval was finally cleared by the early afternoon of the 27th, and Maxse took the decision to delay the assault on the Schwaben Redoubt – the scene of the Ulster Division's heroic stand on 1 July – until 28 September. It duly fell to a well-organized and well-executed attack. 18th

Division's capture of Thiepval reinforced the lesson of Flers and Morval: that careful preparation and training, correct use of artillery, and limited objectives were the key to success.

Unfortunately, the success of 27–28 September could not be maintained. Instead, the fighting on Reserve Army's front (from 1 October to 11 November, formally designated as the battle of the Ancre Heights) reverted to a series of narrow-front, grinding, attritional attacks, aimed at gaining more ground on the Thiepval Ridge. The attacks succeeded, although slowly, and at a high price, for the Germans fought as stubbornly as ever. In early October, von Gallwitz, the commander of Second Army opposite the French, noted that such had been the transfer of his units to First Army, which was faced by relentless British attacks, that his 'only more or less fresh battle reserve' was 'one regiment of the 206th Division; anything else not in the front line is worn out'.[9]

10th Cheshires of 25th Division captured Stuff Redoubt on 9 October. On 1 and 8 October the Canadians attacked the Regina Trench area, between Courcelette and Grandcourt. The Canadians had already attacked in this area, on 15 and 26 September, making little progress. The attack of 1 October suffered from lack of adequate preparation and artillery support. Although 2nd Canadian Division captured most of Kenora Trench, elsewhere the attacks failed with heavy casualties, coming up against uncut barbed wire.

The attack of 21 October was rather more successful. Major General David Watson's 4th Canadian Division, fighting not as part of the Canadian Corps but under the command of Jacob's II Corps, assaulted Regina Trench. The infantry followed a creeping barrage, and mopping-up parties secured the captured positions while the rest of the infantry dug in. German counter-attacks were repelled with the aid of a machine-gun barrage, in which half a million rounds were fired. Undoubtedly, 4th Canadian Division had an advantage in entering the fighting near the end of the Somme offensive, and were thus able to make use of lessons learned the hard way from previous attacks.[10]

That same day another II Corps formation, the British 39th Division, beat off a German counter-attack on the Schwaben – an

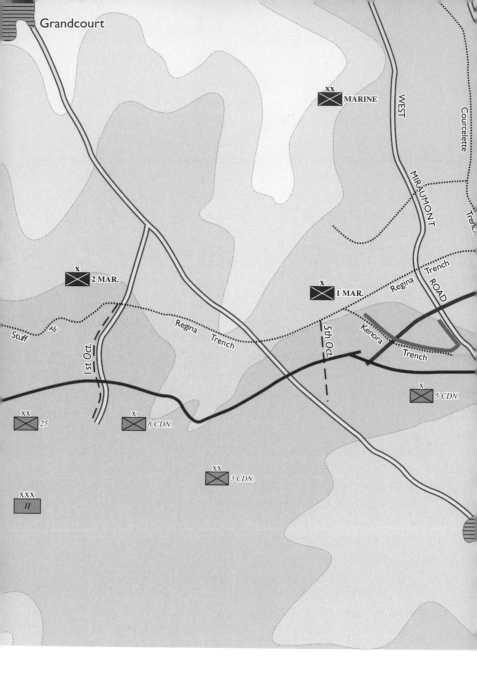

Grandcourt

XX MARINE

WEST

Courcelette

MIRAUMONT

Trench

X 2 MAR.

X 1 MAR.

Regina Trench

ROAD

Stuff Tr.

Regina Trench

Kenora

5th Oct

Trench

1st Oct

X 5 CDN.

XX 25

X 8 CDN.

XX 3 CDN.

XXX II

THE BATTLE OF THE ANCRE HEIGHTS,
1–17 OCTOBER 1916

0   500   1000   1500
Yards

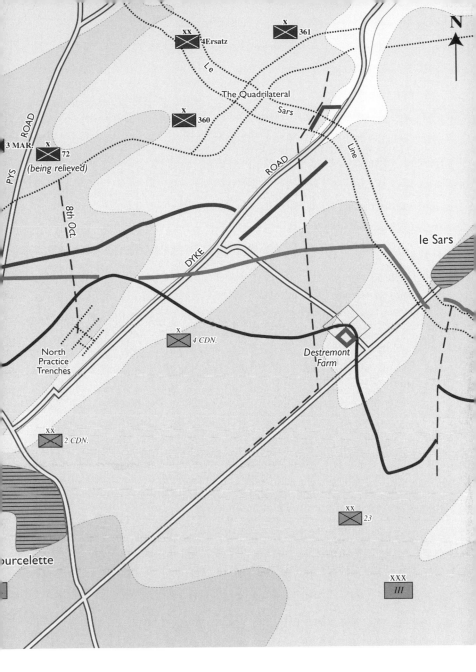

N

XX 4 Ersatz

X 361

Le

The Quadrilateral

Sars

X 360

ROAD

Line

3 MAR.   X 72

(being relieved)

8th Oct.

le Sars

PYS ROAD

DYKE

X 4 CDN.

North
Practice
Trenches

Destremont
Farm

XX 2 CDN.

XX 23

ourcelette

XXX
III

	British line, morning of 1st October
	British line, morning of 2nd October
	British line, morning of 17th October
....	Principal German Trenches

	Land over 140m
	120 – 140m
	100 – 120m
	Land under 100m

indication of how little ground had been gained in a month of severe fighting. 39th Division then moved to the offensive and took Stuff Trench. 18th Division also took some ground, as did 25th Division, despite some units being held up by the British barrage. This Trafalgar Day attack finally delivered the crest of Thiepval Ridge into British hands, but Fifth Army (as Gough's command was renamed at the end of October) was to carry out one last major operation before the battle of the Somme came to an end.

FOURTH ARMY: THE BATTLE OF TRANSLOY RIDGES

The success of the Morval battle gave Haig renewed hope that open warfare was almost within reach. Unfortunately, aerial reconnaissance of the German positions 'revealed the construction of new [defensive] lines consequent to our success. The fourth line had been doubled…a fifth was feverishly being thrown up, in front of Bapaume… and a sixth line had been begun some three miles further east.'[11] To break out into open country would take three Morval-style, limited, set-piece attacks in rapid succession. Such an endeavour was quite simply beyond the capabilities of the BEF in September 1916. Judging by his orders of 29 September, Haig had not grasped this. He planned to bring Allenby's Third Army into the battle in the Gommecourt area, and made ambitious plans for Reserve Army to strike westwards. Rawlinson was to take the German Transloy Line as the first step in an operation that would carry Fourth Army to Cambrai, some 20 miles away.

Initially, things went well. From 1 to 3 October XV and III Corps pushed north, Eaucourt L'Abbaye falling to 47th Division, while 23rd Division (and 2nd Canadian Division of the Canadian Corps) closed up to Le Sars, on the Bapaume road. The weather, which had been fine, then intervened decisively. Heavy rain reduced the ground to a quagmire; Lloyd George later described Passchendaele as 'the battle of the mud', but the same title could easily be applied to the latter stages of the Somme. Poor weather made it difficult to move troops, guns, supplies and tanks forward. Equally damaging was its impact on artillery. When the skies were clear, good aerial observation greatly enhanced the effectiveness of the artillery. On 1 October good weather allowed the RFC to carry out spotting for the guns. The result was impressive. 'As seen from the air,' an RFC pilot noted, 'the barrage appeared a most perfect wall of fire in which it was inconceivable that anything could live.' Infantry of 50th Division '[advanced] close up under the barrage, apparently some 50 yards away from it. They appeared to capture their objective very rapidly and with practically no losses while crossing the open.'[12] This day stood in sharp contrast to the poor weather of later in the month.

Such problems were compounded by the fact that the British were once again attacking up hill – a consequence of their success in capturing the ridge line on 15 September. 'The formation of the ground hid the opposing trenches from view,' explained the historian of 20th (Light) Division. This was

> a factor of great importance, for it made the task of cutting the enemy wire a most difficult one for the artillery. The only point from which a little wire could be seen was close behind our front trenches. The F[orward] O[bservation] O[fficers] and signallers had therefore to lay out and maintain very long telephone wires over fire-swept ground, which owing to the heavy rain of the last few days was little better than a morass.

German machine-guns emerged largely unscathed from the preliminary bombardment, as they had been pulled back to positions out of the range of the British creeping barrage, but still capable of hitting the advancing infantry.[13]

When Rawlinson renewed the attack on 7 October, 23rd Division captured Le Sars with the aid of a tank, but the attacks of 56th, 20th, 12th, 41st and 47th Divisions made only modest progress, and some made none at all. Rawlinson renewed the attack on 12 October, using 4th, 6th, 12th, 30th and 9th Divisions. The British official history of the air war concisely summarized the reason for the failure: 'inadequate artillery preparation due to bad weather and the consequent restriction of air observation'.[14] Yet another attempt was made on 18 October, employing exactly the

The muddy conditions of the latter part of the Somme battle are clearly evident in this photograph of troops in the Ancre Valley in October 1916.

same divisions. This too was largely a failure.

The experiences of a Pals battalion of 30th Division on 18 October can stand for that of all the British infantry during the Transloy Ridges battles. 19th Manchesters took some losses advancing across no man's land, including Second Lieutenant Walker, 'an officer of great merit', who was mortally wounded. 'By the time the Manchesters reached the front line it was apparent that the attack had failed,' although 2nd Wilts, on their flank, had got into the German trenches. A subsequent attack was ordered and then cancelled because a supporting tank had broken down; this was probably just as well, as there was to be 'no special artillery preparation'. Ordered to consolidate, 19th Manchesters were not relieved until the morning of 21 October. The men were 'greatly exhausted', and after heavy rain 'the trenches were in a shockingly bad condition. There were many dead and wounded and several men had completely collapsed, but in spite of their hardships', when the battalion commander went round the Manchesters' positions at 9.00 a.m. on the 20th, 'the remainder were cleaning their rifles, attempting to clear the mud from their trenches and were burying the dead.'[15] The experiences of the Manchesters highlights two important facets of Fourth Army's campaigning in the last two months of the Somme campaign. The first is the hard, unrewarding nature of the fighting. The second is the amazing resilience of the British soldier, which enabled the BEF to survive the Somme campaign with its morale substantially intact.

The prospects for a breakthrough on Fourth Army's front had all but vanished, but still the fighting went on. Rawlinson attacked the Transloy Line again on 23 October with 4th and 8th Divisions; both gained toe-holds in the German positions. Not untypically, one assaulting brigade of each division made modest progress while the other failed. The attack was renewed with a single formation, 33rd Division, on 28 October, with the capture of Rainy Trench resulting. 33rd Division was unable to capitalize on this success, such as it was, when it attacked again on the following day. An order from GHQ to mount a further major attack on the

Transloy Line on 5 November prompted a polite though heartfelt high-level 'mutiny'. Lord Cavan, the commander of XIV Corps, protested in writing to Rawlinson that the task was likely to be futile. It went ahead anyway. It was not a complete fiasco, but the gains were not worth the effort and sacrifice. 33rd Division gained some ground, south of Le Transloy. 1st Australian Division inched forward north of Gueudecourt, only to pull back when it was realized that the positions were untenable. The rain and the mud produced conditions in which the men were 'half-exhausted' before the attack began. A few days later, the commander of 12th (Australian) Brigade, Brigadier General D.J. Glasfurd, was fatally wounded by shellfire. It took ten hours for stretcher-bearers to get him from the front line to an Advanced Dressing Station. Charles Bean, the Australian official historian, went as far as to describe the conditions as 'the worst ever known to the First A.I.F.'[16]

About this time rumours reached Haig's ears that there was a plot to remove him from command of the BEF. Why, then, did Haig persist in attacking in such unfavourable conditions? No doubt his optimism and stubbornness were factors, as was his failure to grasp fully the tactical and operational limitations of fighting in such conditions; but there was more to it than that. A significant factor, perhaps underestimated by some previous historians, was the strait-jacket of coalition warfare. The French remained the senior partners in the coalition, and Joffre, as he wrote to Haig at this time, sought to 'give to our present operations a more decisive form'; to be precise, he wished that 'wide and deep offensive operations should be undertaken without delay in the direction of Achiet-le-Grand, Bapaume, and Bertincourt'. In his reply Haig defended himself against the accusation that he was slackening the BEF's effort:

> Meanwhile to the utmost extent of the means at my disposal, and so far as weather conditions render possible, I will continue to co-operate with you in exploiting to the full the successes already gained. But I must remind you that it lies with me to judge what I can undertake and when I can undertake it. [17]

Haig, in other words, argued for the principle of his being a free agent in committing the BEF to battle, but only within the context of the acceptance that the intense fighting had to continue. French Sixth Army maintained its offensive, and Foch turned down Haig's proposal to pass the relevant sector of the battlefield over to the French so Fayolle could assault Transloy. Haig had little option, whatever his personal preferences, but to carry on attacking alongside Fayolle. By about 6 November, Foch had scaled down his expectations of future operations. This episode is a salutary reminder that the Somme was not a purely British battle but a coalition affair; and it offers support to William Philpott's argument that 'Haig's claim that he mounted and prolonged the Somme battle for the broader interests of the alliance' was fundamentally correct.[18]

This would have been little compensation to the troops who had to endure and attack in this period. The experience of many British units in the battle was summed up by one regimental historian:

> Under the battering-ram system of limited objectives divisions were continually on the move. They were sent into battle, 'used', and taken out to recuperate, absorb drafts (which were very mixed), hold a quiet sector of the line, and then, frequently, moved again into the battle area for further operations.[19]

This was the experience of 50th Division. It went into action on 15 and 26 September and in the Transloy Ridges battle in October. On 5 November this territorial division, largely composed of battalions from the north-east of England, was committed to yet another attack. This time its objective was the Butte de Warlencourt, an ancient burial mound that dominated the battlefield; as Charles Carrington described it: 'a dome of gleaming white chalk from which all vegetation had been blown away by shell fire, it was the most conspicuous object in the landscape by daylight or moonlight'. Like Monte Cassino in a later war, the Butte exercized a powerful and malevolent grip on the minds of the British soldiers crouched in its shadow.[20] First attacked on 6 October, it was assaulted repeatedly but was still in German possession at the end of the battle.

As in so many other episodes of the Somme, on 5 November the assaulting troops made some initial gains but were later driven off. The commander of one of the battalions, 1/9 Durham Light Infantry, was Lieutenant Colonel Roland Boys Bradford. Reflecting on 1/9 DLI's experience, he wrote that

the results that would have been gained in the event of success were of doubtful value. And would have hardly been worth the loss which we would suffer... But the Butte de Warlencourt had become an obsession... So it had to be taken. It seems that the attack was one of those tempting, and unfortunately at one period frequent, local operations which are costly and which are rarely worthwhile. But perhaps that is only the narrow view of the Regimental officer.[21]

Bradford was an outstanding soldier. A pre-war territorial, in November 1916 he was aged just 24. He already held the VC and a year later Bradford was promoted to command a brigade, and killed shortly after. Had he survived, it is entirely conceivable that he would have held high rank in the British Army of the Second World War.

One man who did was Bernard Law Montgomery, who went through the Somme as a junior officer. As a high commander from 1942 to 1945, Montgomery was never afraid to incur heavy casualties in the pursuit of an objective. However, he would only do so if he felt that the objective was truly worth while; and he tried to avoid the piecemeal attacks of the Somme. Instead, he strove to amass overwhelming combat power and land 'colossal cracks' against the enemy.[22] The 'Butte de Warlencourt' syndrome was not entirely absent from Montgomery's army – the fighting for Hill 112 in Normandy was a 1944 version of it – but Roland Boys Bradford's successors had to cope with it less often. That was a legacy of the Somme.

THE FINAL ACT: THE BATTLE OF THE ANCRE

Allied commanders were due to meet for a conference at GQG (Grand Quartier Général – French General Headquarters) in Chantilly on 15–16 November. It would obviously strengthen Haig's hand if the BEF had recently obtained a success. It was against this background that Gough prepared a large-scale offensive to be launched on either side of the River Ancre, in the northern sector of the battlefield. This area had not witnessed major operations since 1 July, and this gave Gough a number of advantages. The terrain, although sodden and muddy, had not been as heavily shelled as that in Fourth Army's sector, and in particular the roads behind the lines were better able to carry traffic. Moreover, the fact that British forward positions were still very much in the same place as they had been in early July shortened the distance that supplies had to be hauled forward. The artillery was largely spared the trials of bringing forward guns over shattered ground, in contrast to the situation south of the Bapaume road. Thus from late September Fourth Army had paid the price of relative success, while on 13 November Fifth Army was to benefit from the catastrophic failure of 1 July.

Gough's plan was essentially limited. Congreve's XIII Corps was to mount a small attack to protect the flank of V Corps (Lieutenant General E.A. Fanshawe). V Corps was to strike on the north bank of the Ancre between Beaucourt and Serre, and advance about 800 yards through the German First Position, which consisted of three or even four trenches. Subsequent objectives would take the troops 1,000 yards further forward. Attacking south of the Ancre between the Schwaben Redoubt and St Pierre Divion, Jacob's II Corps was to secure those parts of the original German front line that remained in the possession of the defenders. If all went well, a number of 1 July objectives, including Serre and Beaumont Hamel, would finally fall to the British. Originally intended for late October, poor weather caused the postponement of the operation on a number of occasions – which strained the nerves of the troops preparing to attack, as a number of memoirists comment – but a period of dry weather enabled Gough to set the attack for 13 November 1916.

Reserve Army had a respectable concentration of artillery, including 282 heavy guns, and a moderately complex creeping barrage was designed to support the infantry. For several days prior to the attack, the artillery bombarded the German positions before first daylight to get the defenders used to a certain pattern of events; this helped to achieve some surprise on the day of the attack. In addition, a 30,000-pound mine was fired under Hawthorn Ridge. This area had of course already been mined on 1 July, and the 13 November explosion produced a double crater. The planning and preparation for the attack was of a generally high standard.

The formation selected by XIII Corps to make a defensive flank to the north of V Corps was 92 Brigade of Major General Wanless-O'Gowan's 31st Division. This was the division that had suffered so grievously at Serre on 1 July, and now, in November, they were committed to battle a few hundred yards away. A couple of battalions got into the German positions, but because the attack of 3rd Division on their flank failed, they were withdrawn. As with the northern Pals battalions in July, the regular and New Army units of Major General C.J. Deverell's 3rd Division were unable to make progress towards Serre. Thick mud and fog hampered the attack, but the major factor was the failure of the British artillery to cut the German barbed wire sufficiently.

The other formations of V Corps fared somewhat better. 2nd Division's attack on Redan Ridge made some progress on 13 November, albeit slowly, but by the following day was roughly level with 51st (Highland) Division. This division was nicknamed 'Harper's Duds', a sobriquet that combined the divisional initials (HD appeared on the divisional insignia), the name of its commander, Major General G.M. Harper, and doubts about its performance earlier in the battle. They had to attack the Beaumont Hamel area, including the sector dominated by the Y-Ravine of infamous memory. Many aspects of 51st Division's assault were strikingly different from 29th Division's attack over the same ground on 1 July. The attack was launched from a trench only 250

Hebuterne

XXX
XIII

X 93

XX 31

X 92

X 76

XX 3

X 8

XX 52

X 6

Serre

Pendant
Copse

XX 2

X 5

XX 12

(relieved by)

XX 208

Redan Ridge

XXX
V

XX 38

XX 51

Hawthorn
Crater

Beaumont
Hamel

(relieved by)

XX 22.

Beaucourt

XX 152

Auchonvillers

Station Rd

Station

X 153

Mound

X 56

St Pierre Divion

XX 63

X 188

X 189

Mill

XX 19.

Hamel

X 118

X 117

XX 39

Menil

Thie

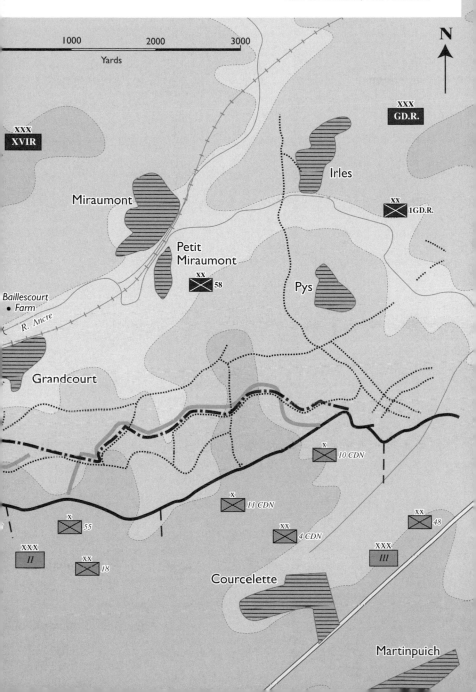

THE BATTLE OF THE ANCRE,
-19 NOVEMBER 1916

————	British line, morning of 13th November
– – – –	Final objective, 13th November
–·–·–	Objective for II Corps, 18th November
▬▬▬▬	Line reached, 14th November
▬▬▬▬	Line consolidated, 19th November

1000   2000   3000
Yards

N

XXX
XVIR

XXX
GD.R.

Irles

Miraumont

XX 1GD.R.

Petit
Miraumont

XX 58

Pys

Baillescourt
• Farm

R. Ancre

Grandcourt

X 10 CDN

X 11 CDN

X 55

XX 48

XX 4 CDN

XXX
II

XXX
III

XX 18

Courcelette

Martinpuich

An officer and NCO of the Machine Gun Corps in the doorway of a captured dugout in Beaumont Hamel, November 1916. The MGC was one of many British specialist units that were created during the war.

or so yards from the German line, rather than the 500 yards that de Lisle's men had had to cover. The Highland Division had the support of an effective barrage, tanks and a machine-gun barrage firing over the heads of the advancing infantry. The result was the capture of Beaumont Hamel, an achievement today commemorated by the 'Jock on the Rock', the divisional memorial which takes the form of a statue of a Highland soldier mounted on a cairn-like pedestal.

On the right of 51st Division, another formation carried out a fine feat of arms by capturing Beaucourt. This was 63rd (Royal Naval) Division, a curious organization that was raised in 1914 largely at the behest of the then First Lord of the Admiralty, Winston Churchill. The RND consisted partly of battalions of the Royal Marine Light Infantry; partly of units of men who were, in theory at least, sailors, although many of them were civilian wartime recruits; and a brigade of 'normal' army battalions. Clinging tenaciously to naval customs such as the wearing of beards, in spite of the army's attempts to make it conform, the RND acquired a unique divisional ethos. The RND was aided by local tactical factors, such as the mist that hampered the German artillery in responding to SOS flares, and tactical surprise, in part founded on 'German complacency' given the apparent impregnability of their positions. However, the weight and effectiveness of the artillery and the skill of the infantry were vital, as were *esprit de corps* and good leadership. The latter was exemplified by the award of a VC to Lieutenant Colonel Bernard Freyberg of the Hood Battalion for displaying inspiring leadership in spite of being wounded three times. Another VC, General de Lisle, called it 'probably the most distinguished personal act of the War'.[23] Freyberg, a New Zealander who had already come to prominence at Gallipoli, later had a distinguished Second World War career as commander of the 2nd New Zealand Division.

V Corps' capture of Beaumont Hamel and Beaucourt were the most notable gains of the battle of the Ancre, but south of the River Ancre Jacob's II Corps also made gains. St Pierre Divion was taken by 39th Division; and 19th Division, which had the butterfly as its symbol, took its objectives with relative ease. Once again, tactical surprise and the infantry keeping close to an effective creeping barrage were identified as important elements in the division's success.

The first phase of the battle of the Ancre was completed by the end of 14 November. It made good tactical sense to complete the capture of Redan Ridge, and Gough was keen to push on. Haig was initially dubious about continuing operations, but was eventually won round, with the result that the battle had a final spasm of activity on 18 November. Rawlinson's Fourth Army had carried out some minor but costly operations in support of the earlier phase of the Ancre offensive, using 2nd Australian Division and elements of 50th Division in the Gird Trench area. Following a German counter-attack, these actions ceased on 16 November. For Fourth Army, the battle of the Somme had ended – at least for the moment. Simultaneously, on 14–15 November the French fought their last major actions of the Somme campaign, at St Pierre Vaast Wood.

Fifth Army's attack on 18 November pushed the line a little further forward on the front of both corps. II Corps used 4th Canadian, 18th and 19th Divisions, Grandcourt proving to be beyond the reach of the latter. On V Corps' front, 37th Division and 32nd Division were used, the latter engaged in a vicious 'battle within a battle' for Frankfort Trench. The battle of the Ancre was a success of sorts. It levered the Germans out of some strong defensive positions, and gave good jumping-off points for renewing the battle when good weather returned in the New Year. Both the British and German Armies were reminded that the BEF had come a long way, tactically, since 1 July. Ludendorff described the battle of the Ancre as 'a particularly heavy blow' which the Germans had thought the British by that stage incapable of launching.[24] Haig was able to go to Chantilly with proof that the British were pulling their weight within the coalition. It was enough; the Allies halted the battle.

CHAPTER 6

THE AFTERMATH

THE CASUALTIES

At the end of the battle of the Somme the Allies had advanced about 7 miles at the price of enormous losses. Exact casualty figures for the campaign are difficult to ascertain. The Germans had a different system of accounting from the British, which makes direct comparisons problematic. Moreover, the British official historian, Sir James Edmonds, has been accused of deliberately inflating German losses to prove that the Somme was a success as a battle of attrition. He suggested a figure of 419,654 British casualties (killed, wounded, missing and prisoners), 204,253 for the French, a total of 623,907 Allied losses, and 680,000 for the Germans. While there is a consensus among historians that Edmonds's figures for Allied losses are correct, his case for those suffered by Germany has been discredited. The Germans themselves claimed to have lost about 500,000 casualties, but that does not include losses during the seven-day preliminary bombardment. Recent historians have disagreed on the total of German losses. Holger Herwig gives a precise 465,000, while Richard Holmes argues that 'it is hard to place them lower than 600,000'.[1] What is clear is that German losses on the Somme dwarfed those sustained at Verdun, roughly 370,000. British losses for the whole year of 1916 amounted to about 660,000. The daily rate of loss for the BEF

during the Somme amounted to 2,943, higher than Third Ypres (Passchendaele) in 1917 (2,323) but significantly lower than the Hundred Days offensive of August–November 1918 (3,645). Worst of all was the battle of Arras in April–May 1917 (4,076). The Somme of course was to witness further fighting after November 1916: 206,104 British soldiers were to die in the *département* of the Somme during the war. An estimated 15–20,000 wounded on the Somme may have died in hospitals elsewhere. Altogether, 127,751 died during the 1916 battle, i.e. from 1 July to 20 November 1916, an average of 893 per day.[2]

REACTIONS IN BRITAIN

Ever since the battle of Mons in August 1914, the British people had been confronted with the reality of heavy casualties. In the year of the Somme, the number of deaths was higher even than at First Ypres, Gallipoli, or Loos. Some reacted with horror. Lord

A Casualty Clearing Station near Albert. These men, the walking wounded, were relatively lucky. Some might even have a coveted 'Blighty wound'.

Landsdowne, a former Foreign Secretary, circulated a private letter among the political élite calling for a compromise peace. A political and social conservative, Landsdowne was fearful of the damage being done to the social structure by the impact of total war. On the other side of the political divide, left-wing anti-war groups redoubled their activities. But these were atypical reactions. The majority of the population grieved, squared their shoulders, and determined to continue the war. In November, a journalist noticed that

> War shrines are now to be seen in the more residential and crowded areas of central London. Usually the shrine is a decorated wooden tablet surmounted by a cross, put up at a street corner, and

containing the names of those from the street who are serving in the Army or Navy, or have been killed in action. There is a ledge for a vase of flowers.

He thought that the appearance of such shrines marked the crumbling of barriers between people in the face of 'the need of mutual aid and comfort in a national emergency'.[3] In Belfast, when the casualty lists from Thiepval were made public, the corporation passed a resolution of congratulation to 36th Division, which had fought 'for the freedom of small nations'.[4]

Suggestions that if the British public had only known the 'truth' about the war the government would have been forced to halt it are ahistorical. Apart from anything else, most civilians knew something of the terrible reality of the war, from soldiers returning on leave, from the sight of blue-clad wounded soldiers on the streets, from graphic letters that appeared in newspapers and from *The Battle of the Somme* feature film. The latter was seen by a sizeable proportion, probably a majority, of the population on the Home Front. The film did not, one soldier thought, 'give you much idea of a bombardment, but casual scenes in and on the way to the trenches are well chosen and amazingly like what happens'.[5] Clearly, the film had a profound emotional impact on civilians who saw it, but it did little to undermine the commitment of the population to the war effort.

The Germans too produced a film: *Heroes on the Somme*. A booklet that accompanied it proclaimed that it depicted 'the German will in war... the German spirit which fights for German honour and German life against enemies that fell upon the German land with the savages of the four quarters of the world' (presumably a reference to the use of non-white colonial troops by the *entente*).[6] The use of propaganda was a hallmark of twentieth-century total warfare; the fact that both sides made films about the Somme is a further indication that the campaign marked an intensification of the struggle.

THE IMPACT OF THE SOMME ON THE
GERMAN ARMY AND STRATEGY

In early December, a German artillery lieutenant stationed on the Somme wrote that 'the aggressive spirit of the French and British still hasn't diminished, even though temporary lulls in the fighting occur, for these serve to enable battle-weary units to be restored to strength and ammunition to be brought forward, and of course, to enable fresh plans of attack to be prepared.'[7] He was right. Fifth Army did indeed carry out some minor but fairly successful operations over the winter, but, in the event, the replacement of Joffre by Nivelle in December 1916 was an important factor in ensuring that the main fighting in 1917 would take place on other parts of the Western Front.

The other factor was that the Germans retreated to the Hindenburg Line. Beginning on 24 February, the Germans abandoned their positions on the Somme battlefield and fell back. As they did so they carried out a methodical scorched-earth policy, leaving a devastated belt of land behind them. Pulling back to the Hindenburg Line undoubtedly handed the German Army some tactical advantages. It shortened the length of front to be held, and put the German troops into a formidable defensive position. But it was also a tacit admission of defeat, that Hindenburg and Ludendorff were not prepared to stand and undergo another attritional struggle on the Somme.

Battered on the Somme, at Verdun, where the French had recaptured much of the ground lost at the beginning of the year, and on the Eastern Front, Ludendorff admitted that 'The Army had been fought to a standstill and was utterly worn out.'[8] Many other Germans believed that the Somme in particular had inflicted heavy damage on their troops. In September the kaiser sent a general to the Somme to discover 'Who was to blame for the repeated defeats of the First Army [opposite the British]?'[9] Captain von Hentig of the Guard Reserve Division described the Somme as the 'muddy grave of the German Army'. Crown Prince Rupprecht of Bavaria stated that 'What remained of the old first-class peace-trained

German infantry had been expended on the battlefield.' Large numbers of experienced soldiers, NCOs and officers were no more. The German Army, as John Terraine has written, had been degraded so that now it, like the BEF, was a 'militia'.[10]

The emergence of Britain as a major military as well as naval and financial power had been a serious blow to the Germans. At the beginning of 1916 they had to reckon with two major enemy armies, the Russian and French. At the end of the year, a third had made its presence felt. The British attacks had been clumsy – First Army reported that 'the British come on in thick masses, some of them drunk' – but they had placed the Germans under enormous strain: 'British pertinacity does not relax.'[11] The situation had looked extremely grim for Germany in July and August, surrounded as it was by enemies. With a little more luck, the BEF could have made some modest but important gains on the Somme, as could French Sixth Army. This would have put the Germans under further pressure. If Romania had entered the war in late June instead of procrastinating until the end of August, it is conceivable that this would have proved one front too many for the Central Powers and their defences would have crumbled some-where, just possibly on the Somme. Certainly the Germans had to strip parts of the Western Front to reinforce the Somme, but Britain's lack of reserves and logistic problems meant that the BEF could not take advantage of this by attacking elsewhere.[12]

At the end of 1916 the German military leadership was under no illusion about what was likely to come next. In Ludendorff's words the German High Command had to

> bear in mind that the enemy's great superiority in men and material would be even more painfully felt in 1917 than in 1916. They had to face the danger that 'Somme fighting' would soon break out at various points on our fronts, and that even our troops would not be able to withstand such attacks indefinitely, especially if the enemy gave us no time for rest and for the accumulation of material.[13]

This bleak but realistic prognosis led to the recognition that Germany could not win the war on the Western Front in 1917.

Instead, the German élite decided to seek victory by waging unrestricted submarine warfare in an attempt to starve Britain into submission by cutting its Atlantic lifeline. This strategy not only failed to achieve its objective, but brought the United States into the war, with consequences that were ultimately disastrous for Germany.

THE IMPACT OF THE SOMME ON THE BRITISH ARMY AND STRATEGY

The Somme shattered the strategic consensus in Britain. David Lloyd George, who became Prime Minister in December 1916, believed that the Somme was 'a ghastly failure' and in 1917 manoeuvred against Haig and Robertson, seeking to subordinate the BEF to the new French C-in-C, Nivelle, and trying to get the main Allied effort shifted to the Italian front. A spirit of deep pessimism, even defeatism, infected much of the British élite, with the notable exception of Haig. The Somme, where the resources of the entire empire had strained in vain to force a way through the German lines, seemed to show that victory was as far away as ever. However, the gains of the Somme in terms of coalition politics were considerable. In four and a half months of bloody fighting, Britain had demonstrated to its allies its willingness to pay the blood tax, to play a leading role in taking on the main enemy in the main theatre of operations.

On the battlefield, the picture was somewhat rosier. The British Army was a far more effective instrument of war in November 1916 than it had been in July. In contrast to the Germans, the British lost mainly inexperienced troops while the survivors had, in a strictly military sense, benefited greatly from the experience. British morale remained good, although the enthusiasm of the summer had been replaced by grim determination. The experience of the Somme was widely spread among British troops, as fifty-three of the fifty-six divisions of the BEF fought in the battle.

The pay-off of the lessons of the Somme did not come until spring 1917, when the BEF mounted its next major offensive, this

THE END OF THE BATTLE

 Front line, 1st July

Front line at end of battle

x x x x x Franco-British boundary

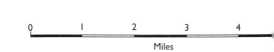

0   1   2   3   4

Miles

time around Arras with Allenby's Third Army in the van. The opening day of the battle, 9 April 1917, was in some ways comparable with 1 July 1916. On both occasions the BEF committed fourteen divisions along a broadly similar frontage (Arras was in fact a little shorter). Both battles began with a prolonged preliminary bombardment. By contrast, the density of heavy guns was three times greater at Arras than on the Somme. Ammunition was more plentiful (although not unlimited) and more reliable. Effective counter-battery work ensured the silencing of a high proportion of German guns. The infantry had reorganized and trained according to official pamphlets S.S.143 and S.S.144 that encapsulated the tactical lessons of the Somme.

By the end of 9 April 1917 the BEF had won a major victory. Canadian Corps of First Army captured Vimy Ridge, and elsewhere British divisions made substantial advances, including the 3 1/2 miles achieved by 4th and 9th Divisions – the longest single advances made under the conditions of trench warfare up to that date. This is evidence of an army that had learned from the Somme, and had applied those lessons to good effect. The BEF still had a long way to go. The first day of Arras proved that it was effective at fighting a set-piece battle, but subsequent days would demonstrate that it still had much to learn about conducting mobile operations. But given the inexperience of the citizen army only months before, the level of tactical and operational development demonstrated at Arras was substantial. The Arras method would be refined throughout 1917 and 1918, until by the final Hundred Days campaign of 1918 it had become a battle-winning formula to which, when properly applied, the Germans had no answer. This method can ultimately be traced to the trial and error days on the Somme.

The Somme left Haig more convinced than ever that the morale of the German Army had been seriously eroded, as had its reserves. Haig's *Final Dispatch*, written in 1919, constituted a defence of his conduct of the war. His key argument was that the victory of 1918 had been made possible by the attritional battles of 1915–17. In a striking phrase, Haig described the fighting on the Western Front as 'one great and continuous engagement', which conformed to the pre-war idea of phased battle. In his dispatch dated 23 December 1916, Haig dubbed the Somme as the 'Opening of the Wearing-Out Battle'. Haig's dispatches contain some *ex post facto* rationalization, but that is not to say that his case was entirely wrong. The dreadful battles of attrition undoubtedly undermined the German Army's willingness and ability to fight, but it proved much more resilient than Haig had anticipated. For the Allies, the Somme was not a 'victory' in the traditional sense, but it was certainly a success. Moreover, it is difficult to avoid the conclusion that the battle of the Somme was an essential precondition to the Allied victory of 1918.

BRITISH GENERALSHIP ON THE SOMME

Today, much of the popular condemnation of the British generalship in the First World War is based on the example of the Somme, especially the first day; indeed, few other than specialist military historians bother to look much beyond 1 July. This seems to be a relatively recent development. Much of the case against Haig levelled by the likes of Lloyd George and Liddell Hart in the 1920s and 1930s was based on the Third Battle of Ypres (Passchendaele) in 1917, rather than the Somme. Ironically, some modern historians, myself included, are more inclined to look favourably on the BEF's tactical and operational performance during Third Ypres than on the Somme. It might be the case that 1 July 1916 only took on its iconic status in the 1960s, when there was a significant revival of interest in the Great War.

While much criticism of British generalship on the Somme is superficial and trite, there is undoubtedly a case to answer. Haig overestimated the ability of his army in July 1916, in effect trying to make an infant force run before it could properly walk. His objectives were over-ambitious, a fault that was also true of his plans for 15 September, and for the attack of 7 October. Rawlinson certainly had the right idea with his notion of limited, 'bite and hold' actions, but on 1 July and again on the 14th failed to have an effective 'Plan B' if an opportunity for a substantial advance

German dead on the Somme; the man in the centre appears to have his hands tied together. One part of the grim arithmetic of war, German casualty figures for the battle, are still disputed.

occurred. Haig was inconsistent in his behaviour towards his subordinates. He sometimes overrode the judgement of the man on the spot, as in the planning for 15 September, but did not always exercise sufficient control over Rawlinson and Gough, or the corps commanders, when they failed to co-ordinate attacks. Haig at various times gave Rawlinson advice and even instructions on how he should command his army, but overall his approach lacked consistency and 'grip'. Most puzzling of all is the inability of Haig and Rawlinson consistently to apply the lessons of successful attacks such as 14 and 27 July, especially the importance of careful preparation and massed artillery. However, the success of the battle of the Ancre indicated that Gough, whose previous 'thrusting', narrow-front attacks have rightly been much criticized, at least had learned something. On the credit side, Haig kept his nerve during the Somme offensive and ensured that the BEF delivered a series of body blows to the German Army. In retrospect, it was unrealistic to expect the amateur and inexperienced BEF of 1916 to do much more than this, although clearly it could have performed more effectively at the tactical and operational levels.

In 1917 General Sir Herbert Plumer, commander of Second Army, emerged as an outstanding practitioner of the bite and hold method of battle. His victories at Messines (June 1917) and his conduct of the middle phase of Third Ypres demonstrated his mastery of the set-piece battle, based on careful preparation, co-ordination of attacks, and an understanding of the importance of achievable, limited objectives. In the circumstances of 1916, he might seem a better choice of C-in-C than Haig, and certainly preferable as an army commander to Gough and perhaps even Rawlinson. However, as we have seen, Haig was far more than simply an Army Group commander, and it is not clear whether Plumer possessed the aptitude to fulfil all of Haig's roles. A more sensible command structure might have placed Plumer as operational commander, directly supervising the armies, under Haig as theatre commander, much as in the Second World War Alexander was C-in-C Middle East with Montgomery as his operational commander. Haig simply had too much to do. The problem with this piece of fantasy was that Plumer's relations with Haig in 1916 were by no means good. Haig had come close to sacking Plumer in February 1916 over an incident in the Ypres Salient. The 'old man', as Haig referred to Plumer – in fact, Plumer was only four years older than the C-in-C – was still on trial in July 1916. Finally, in 1917 Plumer had the advantage of learning from the experiences of the previous year.

It is possible, although unlikely, that the other potential C-in-C and Army commanders of 1916 would have been an improvement on Haig and Rawlinson. There is too little evidence on which to judge the suitability of Monro, commander of First Army. At the battle of Arras in 1917, Allenby showed the limitations of his understanding of the nature of combat on the Western Front, but on the Somme he would probably have done no worse and quite possibly rather better than Gough. Of the five army commanders of 1916, two were still in place during the victorious autumn campaign of 1918. These were Plumer and Rawlinson, commanders of Second and Fourth Armies respectively. The other three army commanders in late 1918 had all commanded corps on the Somme two years earlier. Byng's conduct of operations in 1916–17, as Canadian Corps and then Third Army commander, suggests that he might have acquitted himself well on the Somme in place of Gough or even Rawlinson. With less certainty, one can say the same of Horne, XV Corps commander on the Somme but appointed to command First Army late in 1916, when Monro went to become C-in-C in India. The record of the Fifth Army commander in the Hundred Days, Birdwood, was patchier. Two men who proved to be outstanding commanders in the 1918 Advance to Victory were in July 1916 largely untried, and in any case too junior. These were Arthur Currie (1st Canadian Division) and John Monash (3rd Australian Division – this formation saw little fighting on the Somme). The fact that both were 'colonials' and not professional soldiers would have probably militated against appointment to higher command in 1916.

Just as in the British Army of the Second World War, between 1914 and 1918 a rough meritocracy of commanders emerged in the BEF at all levels. Haig was probably lucky not to be C-in-C BEF in 1914–15. Struggling with limited resources against a powerful enemy, he would probably have gone the way of Sir John French, or Lord Gort (C-in-C BEF 1939–40). Instead, Haig, like Bernard Montgomery a generation later, had the good fortune to come to high command at a time when the army was beginning to receive resources – men, munitions and weapons – in abundance. But Haig was more than just lucky. He was a skilful practitioner of modern warfare. In 1916–17 Haig oversaw the professionalization of the BEF, in areas such as logistics, training schools, dissemination of tactical lessons through the production of official pamphlets (the 'S.S. series'), staff work and the like. Improvements in administration and infrastructure were vital elements in the learning curve that transformed the BEF from the clumsy organization of July 1916 to the formidable army of August 1918. In effect, Haig, and also Rawlinson, served their apprenticeship as higher commanders on the Somme. Both were to perform more effectively in the campaigns to come.

THE SOMME SINCE 1916

By the standards of the Western Front, 1917 was a quiet year on the Somme. There was a certain amount of raiding, much shelling and some minor operations; minor, that is, in comparison to those of 1916, but still highly dangerous for those who took part. The main focus of attention switched to the south for the French for the Nivelle offensive of May 1917, and north for the BEF for the battles of Arras (April–May), Third Ypres (July–November) and Cambrai (November–December). In March 1918 war once again came to the Somme, as a major German offensive broke through the British lines and some British defenders retreated back over the 1916 battlefield. One of the many victims of the German spring offensive was Brigadier General R. Barnett-Barker of 99 Brigade, 2nd Division, who was killed by a shell on 24 March. He was killed in Gueudecourt, barely 3 miles from Delville Wood, where as a lieutenant colonel he had commanded the 22nd Royal Fusiliers in the successful attack of 27 July 1916. On 21 August 1918 British Third and Fourth Armies began an offensive that was to recapture Albert, lost in the spring, take the BEF across the 1916 battlefield, and result in the seizure of Bapaume and Péronne, both of which had eluded the grasp of the BEF in the 1916 campaign. All of this occurred in just two weeks, a fact indicative of changes both in the nature of the fighting and the efficiency of the British Army since the first battle of the Somme.

After the war, the Somme countryside gradually returned to normal, although the landscape was now dotted with British military cemeteries, 242 in all in the Somme *département*. They ranged in size from the largest, Serre Road No. 2 (7,139 graves) to Hunter's Cemetery, one of the smallest, with only 46 burials. In all, the Somme cemeteries contain 153,040 British graves. 99,631 bodies were identified and 53,409 contained the remains of unknown soldiers. The Thiepval Memorial to the Missing, inaugurated in 1932, contains the names of 73,357 soldiers recorded as 'missing', with no known grave. At Caterpillar Valley cemetery, a memorial to missing New Zealanders records a further 1,205 names. Bodies are still being unearthed.[14] To this day, the Commonwealth (formerly Imperial) War Graves Commission maintains the numerous cemeteries in immaculate order.

The British also built over 100 memorials. The largest, the building-block-style Memorial to the Missing at Thiepval, can be seen over a good part of the northern sector of the battlefield and is unfortunately rather ugly. Many divisions and regiments erected memorials after the war. Many took the form of crosses like that of the 16th (Irish) Division at Guillemont, or obelisks (1st Australian Division, Pozières). Some were a little more imaginative: the statue of the soldier in fighting order at Flers (41st Division) or the Ulster Tower at Thiepval, modelled on one located on 36th Division's training ground in Northern Ireland. The Somme was a place of pilgrimage in the 1920s and 1930s, as veterans and their families returned to visit the old battlefields, to lay wreaths in cemeteries, to honour their dead.

War returned to the Somme in 1940. The German *panzers* crossed the 1916 battlefield on their drive to the Channel. A British battalion, 7th Royal West Kents, which in a previous incarnation had been part of Maxse's 18th Division, was destroyed in the defence of Albert on 20 May 1940. The sheer speed of the German advance meant that the Somme was not subjected to fighting of the intensity of 1916 or 1918. The same was true in September 1944, when the Allies, having broken out of Normandy, crossed the Somme area from the other direction. Guards Armoured Division raced down the Serre Road, past the Great War cemeteries. They had plenty of fighting ahead of them but little of it was on the Somme.

The reality of a battle of attrition: British battlefield burials near Carnoy, July 1916. After the war, the Imperial War Graves Commission replaced temporary crosses with permanent headstones.

Today, the Somme receives more British visitors than ever before. Over the last thirty years there has been a huge revival of interest in the battle, for which Martin Middlebrook's 1971 book *The First Day on the Somme* can claim much credit. Most visitors go to the sites of 1 July 1916, far fewer to places associated with the later fighting, and fewer still to the places fought over in 1918. The Newfoundland battlefield park, where 29th Division's trenches have been allowed to be grassed over, attracts large numbers of visitors, many of them parties of British school children. Memorials are still being erected, evidence of a fascination with the First World War that shows no sign of abating in the early twenty-first century. One of the most impressive modern ones is the red dragon clutching barbed wire in its talons and glaring towards Mametz Wood, the scene of 38th (Welsh) Division's actions in July 1916.

The Somme battlefield today is a tranquil place, the countryside a pleasure to walk over. Looking at the peaceful hills and woods, fields and villages, it is easy to forget that one of the most terrible battles in British history was fought there, just within living memory. The horror of the battle should not blind us to its importance. 'The Somme' is indelibly branded on the British psyche as an unredeemed disaster. This view does not accord with historical evidence. A Somme veteran captured the reality neatly when he wrote:

> Only high hearts, splendid courage and the enormous endurance of the flower of the nations of the British and French Empires engaged could have won the results attained. Only wonderful powers of resistance by the Germans could have limited them to what they were.[15]

The battle of the Somme was not a victory in itself, but without it the *entente* would not have emerged victorious in 1918.

The Thiepval Memorial to the Missing. In front of the Memorial is a joint Anglo-French cemetery, symbolic of the two nations united in sacrifice.

APPENDIX A

ORDER OF BATTLE OF THE BEF ON THE SOMME

British Expeditionary Force – General Sir Douglas Haig

Fourth Army – General Sir Henry Rawlinson
Reserve/Fifth Army – General Sir Hubert Gough
Third Army – General Sir Edmund H.H. Allenby

II Corps – Lieutenant General C.W. Jacob
III Corps – Lieutenant General Sir W.P. Pulteney
V Corps – Lieutenant General E.A. Fanshawe
VII Corps – Lieutenant General Sir T. d'O Snow
VIII Corps – Lieutenant General Sir A.G. Hunter-Weston
X Corps – Lieutenant General Sir T.L.N. Morland
XIII Corps – Lieutenant General Sir W.N. Congreve
XIV Corps – Lieutenant General The Earl of Cavan
XV Corps – Lieutenant General H.S. Horne (promoted to command First Army) then Lieutenant General J.P. du Cane
I Anzac – Lieutenant General Sir W.R. Birdwood
Canadian Corps – Lieutenant General the Honourable Sir J. Byng

Guards Division

Major General G.P.T. Feilding

1st Guards Brigade
2/Grenadier Guards, 2/Coldstream Guards,
3/Coldstream Guards, 1/Irish Guards
2nd Guards Brigade
3/Grenadier Guards, 1/Coldstream Guards,
1/Scots Guards, 2/Irish Guards
3rd Guards Brigade
1/Grenadier Guards, 4/Grenadier Guards,
2/Scots Guards, 1/Welch Guards
Pioneers: 4/Coldstream Guards

1st Division

Major General E.P. Strickland

1st Brigade
10/Glosters, 1/Black Watch,
8/Royal Berkshires, 1/Camerons
2nd Brigade
2/Royal Sussex, 1/Loyal North Lancashire,
1/Northamptons, 2/King's Royal Rifle
Corps
3rd Brigade
1/South Wales Borderers, 1/Glosters,
2/Welch, 2/Royal Munster Fusiliers
Pioneers: 1/6th Welch

2nd Division

Major General W.G. Walker

5th Brigade
17/Royal Fusiliers, 24/Royal Fusiliers,
2/Oxfordshire and Buckinghamshire Light
Infantry, 2/Highland Light Infantry
6th Brigade
1/King's, 2/South Staffordshires,
13/Essex, 17/Middlesex
99th Brigade
22/Royal Fusiliers, 23/Royal Fusiliers,
1/Royal Berkshires, 1/King's Royal Rifle
Corps
Pioneers: 10/Duke of Cornwall's Light
Infantry

3rd Division

Major General J.A. Haldane
(promoted to command VI Corps)
then Major General C.J. Deverell
8th Brigade
2/Royal Scots, 8/East Yorkshires

1/Royal Scots Fusiliers
7/King's Shropshire Light Infantry
9th Brigade
1/Northumberland Fusiliers
4/Royal Fusiliers, 13/King's Regiment
12/West Yorkshires
76th Brigade
8/King's Own, 2/Suffolks
10/Royal Welch, 1/Gordons
Pioneers: 20/King's Royal Rifle Corps

4th Division

Major General the Honourable W.
Lambton
1/Royal Warwicks, 2/Seaforths
1/Royal Irish Fusiliers
2/Royal Dublin Fusiliers
11th Brigade
1/Somerset Light Infantry
1/East Lancashires, 1/Hampshires
1/Rifle Brigade
12th Brigade
1/King's Own, 2/Lancashire Fusiliers
2/Essex, 2/Duke of Wellington's
Pioneers: 21/West Yorkshires

5th Division

Major General R.B. Stephens

13th Brigade
14/Royal Warwicks, 15/Royal Warwicks
2/King's Own Scottish Borderers
1/Royal West Kents
15th Brigade
16/Royal Warwicks, 1/Norfolks
1/Bedfords, 1/Cheshires
95th Brigade
1/Devons, 12/Glosters, 1/East Surreys
1/Duke of Cornwall's Light Infantry
Pioneers: 1/6th Argyll and Sutherlands

6th Division

Major General C. Ross

16th Brigade
1/Buffs (Royal East Kent), 8/Bedfords
1/King's Shropshire Light Infantry
2/York and Lancaster
18th Brigade
1/West Yorkshires, 11/Essex
2/Durham Light Infantry

14/Durham Light Infantry
71st Brigade
9/Norfolks, 9/Suffolks
1/Leicesters, 2/Sherwood Foresters
Pioneers: 11/Leicesters

7th Division

Major General H.E. Watts
20th Brigade
8/Devons, 9/Devons
2/Borders, 2/Gordons
22nd Brigade
2/Royal Warwicks, 2/Royal Irish
1/Royal Welch Fusiliers, 20/Manchesters
91st Brigade
2/Queen's, 1/South Staffordshires
21/Manchesters, 22/Manchesters
Pioneers: 24/Manchesters

8th Division

Major General H. Hudson
23rd Brigade
2/Devons, 2/West Yorkshires
2/Middlesex, 2/Scots Rifles
24th Brigade[1]
1/Worcestershires, 1/Sherwood Foresters
2/Northamptons, 2/East Lancashires
25th Brigade
2/Lincolns, 2/Royal Berkshires
1/Royal Irish Rifles, 2/Rifle Brigade
Pioneers: 22/Durham Light Infantry

9th (Scottish) Division

Major General W.T. Furse
26th Brigade
8/Black Watch, 7/Seaforths, 5/Camerons
10/Argyll and Sutherlands
27th Brigade
11/Royal Scots, 12/Royal Scots
6/King's Own Scottish Borderers
9/Scottish Rifles
South African Brigade
1/ Cape Province, 2/Natal & O.F.S.
3/Transvaal and Rhodesia, 4/Scottish
Pioneers: 9/Seaforth

11th Division

Lieutenant General Sir C.
Woollcombe

32nd Brigade
9/West Yorkshires, 6/Green Howards
8/Duke of Wellington's
6/York and Lancaster
33rd Brigade
6/Lincolns, 6/Borders
7/South Staffordshires
9/Sherwood Foresters
34th Brigade
8/Northumberland Fusiliers
9/Lancashire Fusiliers
5/Dorsets, 11/Manchesters
Pioneers: 6/East Yorkshires

12th Division

Major General A.B. Scott
35th Brigade
7/Norfolks, 7/Suffolks
9/Essex, 5/Royal Berkshires
36th Brigade
8/Royal Fusiliers, 9/Royal Fusiliers
7/Royal Sussex, 11/Middlesex
37th Brigade
6/Queen's, 6/Buffs
7/East Surreys, 6/Royal West Kents
Pioneers: 5/Northamptons

14th (Light) Division

Major General V.A. Couper
41st Brigade
7/King's Royal Rifle Corps
8/King's Royal Rifle Corps
7/Rifle Brigade, 8/Rifle Brigade
42nd Brigade
5/Oxfordshire and Buckinghamshire Light
  Infantry
5/King's Shropshire Light Infantry
9/King's Royal Rifle Corps
9/Rifle Brigade
43rd Brigade
6/Somerset Light Infantry
6/Duke of Cornwall's Light Infantry
6/King's Own Yorkshire Light Infantry
10/Durham Light Infantry
Pioneers: 11/King's

15th (Scottish) Division

Major General F.W.N. McCracken
44th Brigade
9/Black Watch, 8/Seaforths
8th/10th Gordons, 7/Camerons

45th Brigade
13/Royal Scottish
6th/7th Royal Scots Fusiliers, 6/Camerons
11/Argyll and Sutherlands
46th Brigade
10/Scottish Rifle
7th/8th King's Own Scottish Borderers
10th/11th Highland Light Infantry
12/Highland Light Infantry
Pioneers: 9/Gordons

16th (Irish) Division

Major General W.B. Hickie
47th Brigade
6/Royal Irish, 6/Connaught Rangers
7/Leinster, 8/Royal Munster Fusiliers
48th Brigade
7/Royal Irish Rifles
1/Royal Munster Fusiliers
8/Royal Dublin Fusiliers
9/Royal Dublin Fusiliers
49th Brigade
7/Royal Inniskilling Fusiliers
8/Royal Inniskilling Fusiliers
7/Royal Irish Fusiliers
8/Royal Irish Fusiliers
Pioneers: 11/Hampshires

17th Division

Major General T.D. Pilcher (relieved)
then Major General P.R. Robertson
50th Brigade
10/West Yorkshires, 7/East Yorkshires
7/Green Howards, 6/Dorsets
51st Brigade
7/Lincolns, //Borders
8/South Staffordshires
10/Sherwood Foresters
52nd Brigade
9/Northumberland Fusiliers
10/Lancashire Fusiliers
9/Duke of Wellington's
12/Manchesters
Pioneers: 7/York and Lancaster

18th (Eastern) Division

Major General F.I. Maxse
53rd Brigade
8/Norfolks, 8/Suffolks
10/Essex, 6/Royal Berkshires

54th Brigade
11/Royal Fusiliers, 7/Bedfords
6/Northamptons, 12/Middlesex
55th Brigade
7/Queen's, 7/Buffs
8/East Surreys, 7/Royal West Kents
Pioneers: 8/Royal Sussex

19th (Western) Division

Major General G.T.M. Bridges
56th Brigade
7/King's Own, 7/East Lancashires
7/South Lancashires, 7/Loyal North
Lancashires
57th Brigade
10/Royal Warwicks, 8/Glosters
10/Worcestershires, 8/North Staffordshires
58th Brigade
9/Cheshires, 9/Royal Welch Fusiliers
9/Welch, 6/Wiltshires
Pioneers: 5/South Wales Borderers

20th (Light) Division

Major General W.D. Smith
59th Brigade
10/King's Royal Rifle Corps
11/King's Royal Rifle Corps
10/Rifle Brigade, 11/Rifle Brigade
60th Brigade
6/Oxford and Buckinghamshire Light
  Infantry
6/King's Shropshire Light Infantry
12/King's Royal Rifle Corps
12/Rifle Brigade
61st Brigade
7/Somerset Light Infantry
7/Duke of Cornwall's Light Infantry
7/King's Own Yorkshire Light Infantry
12/King's
Pioneers: 11/Durham Light Infantry

21st Division

Major General D.G.M. Campbell
62nd Brigade
12/Northumberland Fusiliers
13/Northumberland Fusiliers
1/Lincolns, 10/Green Howards
63rd Brigade[2]
8/Lincolns, 8/Somerset Light Infantry
4/Middlesex, 10/York and Lancaster

64th Brigade
1/East Yorkshires
9/King's Own Yorkshire Light Infantry
10/King's Own Yorkshire Light Infantry
15/Durham Light Infantry
Pioneers: 14/Northumberland Fusiliers

23rd Divison

Major General J.M. Babington
68th Brigade
10/Northumberland Fusiliers
11/Northumberland Fusiliers
12/Durham Light Infantry
13/Durham Light Infantry
69th Brigade
11/West Yorkshires, 8/Green Howards
9/Green Howards
10/Duke of Wellington's
70th Brigade[3]
11/Sherwood Foresters
8/King's Own Yorkshire Light Infantry
8/York and Lancaster, 9/York and Lancaster
Pioneers: 9/South Staffordshires

24th Division

Major General J.E. Capper
17th Brigade
8/Buffs, 1/Royal Fusiliers
12/Royal Fusiliers, 3/Rifle Brigade
72nd Brigade
8/Queen's, 9/East Surreys
8/Royal West Kents, 1/North Staffordshires
73rd Brigade
9/Royal Sussex, 7/Northamptons
13/Middlesex, 2/Leinsters
Pioneers: 12/Sherwood Foresters

25th Division

Major General E.G.T. Bainbridge
7th Brigade
10/Cheshires, 3/Worcesters
8/Loyal North Lancashires, 1/Wiltshires
74th Brigade
11/Lancashire Fusiliers, 13/Cheshires
9/Loyal North Lancashires
2/Royal Irish Rifles
75th Brigade
11/Cheshires, 8/Borders
2/South Lancashires, 8/South Lancashires
Pioneers: 6/South Wales Borderers

29th Division

Major General H. de b. de Lisle
86th Brigade
2/Royal Fusiliers, 1/Lancashire Fusiliers
16/Middlesex, 1/Royal Dublin Fusiliers
87th Brigade
2/South Wales Borderers
1/King's Own Scottish Borderers
1/Royal Inniskilling Fusiliers
1/Borders
88th Brigade
4/Worcestershires, 1/Essex
2/Hampshires
Royal Newfoundland Regiment
Pioneers: 2/Monmouths

30th Division

Major General J.S.M. Shea
21st Brigade
18/King's, 2/Green Howards
2/Wiltshires, 19/Manchesters
89th Brigade
17/King's, 19/King's, 20/King's, 2/Bedfords
90th Brigade
2/Royal Scots Fusiliers, 16/Manchesters
17/Manchesters, 18/Manchesters
Pioneers: 11/South Lancashires

31st Division

Major General R. Wanless O'Gowan
92nd Brigade
10/East Yorkshires, 11/East Yorkshires
12/East Yorkshires, 13/East Yorkshires
93rd Brigade
15/West Yorkshires, 16/West Yorkshires
18/West Yorkshires
18/Durham Light Infantry
94th Brigade
11/East Lancashires, 12/York and Lancaster
13/York and Lancaster
14/York and Lancaster
Pioneers: 12/King's Own Yorkshire Light
Infantry

32nd Division

Major General W.H. Rycroft
14th Brigade
19/Lancashire Fusiliers[4], 1/Dorsetshires
2/Manchesters, 15/Highland Light Infantry

96th Brigade
16/Northumberland Fusiliers
15/Lancashire Fusiliers
16/Lancashire Fusiliers
2/Royal Inniskilling Fusiliers
97th Brigade
11/Borders
2/King's Own Yorkshire Light Infantry
16/Highland Light Infantry
17/Highland Light Infantry
Pioneers: 17/Northumberland Fusiliers[5]

33rd Division

Major General H.J.S. Landon then
Major General R.J. Pinney
19th Brigade
20th Royal Fusiliers
2/Royal Welch Fusiliers
1/Cameronians, 5/Scottish Rifles
98th Brigade
4/King's, 1/4th Suffolks
1/Middlesex
2/Argyll and Sutherlands
100th Brigade
1/Queen's, 2/Worcestershires
16/King's Royal Rifle Corps
1/9th Highland Light Infantry
Pioneers: 18/Middlesex

34th Division

Major General E.C. Ingouville-
Williams (killed) then Major General
C.L. Nicholson
101st Brigade
15/Royal Scots, 16/Royal Scots
10/Lincolns, 11/Suffolks
102nd (Tyneside Scottish) Brigade[6]
20/Northumberland Fusiliers
21/ Northumberland Fusiliers
22/Northumberland Fusiliers
23/ Northumberland Fusiliers
103rd (Tyneside Irish) Brigade[7]
24/ Northumberland Fusiliers
25/ Northumberland Fusiliers
26/ Northumberland Fusiliers
27/ Northumberland Fusiliers
Pioneers: 18/ Northumberland Fusiliers[8]

35th (Bantam) Division

Major General R.J. Pinney
104th Brigade

17/Lancashire Fusiliers
18/Lancashire Fusiliers
20/Lancashire Fusiliers, 23/Manchesters
105th Brigade
15/Cheshire, 16/Cheshire
14/Glosters, 15/Sherwood Foresters
106th Brigade
17/Royal Scots, 17/West Yorkshires
19/Durham Light Infantry
18/Highland Light Infantry
Pioneers: 19/Northumberland Fusiliers

36th (Ulster) Division

Major General O.S.W. Nugent
107th Brigade
8/Royal Irish Rifles, 9/Royal Irish Rifles
10/Royal Irish Rifles, 15/Royal Irish Rifles
108th Brigade
11/Royal Irish Rifles, 12/Royal Irish Rifles
13/Royal Irish Rifles, 9/Royal Irish Fusiliers
109th Brigade
9/Royal Inniskilling Fusiliers
10/ Royal Inniskilling Fusiliers
11/ Royal Inniskilling Fusiliers
14/Royal Irish Rifles
Pioneers: 16/Royal Irish Rifles

37th Divison

Major General S.W. Scrase-Dickens
(sick) then Major General H.B.
Williams
110th Brigade[9]
6/Leicesters, 7/Leicesters
8/Leicesters, 9/Leicesters
111th Brigade[10]
10/Royal Fusiliers, 13/Royal Fusiliers
13/King's Royal Rifle Corps
13/Rifle Brigade
112th Brigade[11]
11/Royal Warwicks, 6/Bedfords
8/East Lancashires
10/Loyal North Lancashires
Pioneers: 9/North Staffordshires[12]

38th (Welsh) Division

Major General I. Philipps (relieved)
then Major General C.G. Blackader
113th Brigade
13/Royal Welch Fusiliers
14/Royal Welch Fusiliers
15/Royal Welch Fusiliers

16/Royal Welch Fusiliers
114th Brigade
10/Welch, 13/Welch, 14/Welch, 15/Welch
115th Brigade
10/South Wales Borderers
11/South Wales Borderers
17/Royal Welch Fusiliers, 16/Welch
Pioneers: 19/Welch

39th Division

Major General G.J. Cuthbert

116th Brigade
11/Royal Sussex, 12/Royal Sussex
13/Royal Sussex, 14/Hampshires
117th Brigade
16/Sherwood Foresters
17/Sherwood Foresters
17/King's Royal Rifle Corps
16/Rifle Brigade
118th Brigade
1/6th Cheshires, 1/1st Cambridgeshires
1/1st Hertfordshires, 4th/5th Black Watch
Pioneers: 13/Glosters

41st Division

Major General S.T.B. Lawford

122nd Brigade
12/East Surreys, 15/Hampshires
11/Royal West Kents
18/King's Royal Rifle Corps
123rd Brigade
11/Queen's, 10/Royal West Kents
23/Middlesex, 20/Durham Light Infantry
124th Brigade
10/Queen's, 26/Royal Fusiliers
32/Royal Fusiliers
21/King's Royal Rifle Corps
Pioneers: 19/Middlesex

46th (North Midland) Division (T.F.)

Major General Hon. E.J. Montagu-
Stuart-Wortley (relieved) then Major
General W. Thwaites

137th Brigade
1/5th South Staffordshires
1/6th South Staffordshires
1/5th North Staffordshires
1/6th North Staffordshires
138th Brigade
1/4th Lincolns, 1/5th Lincolns

1/4th Leicesters, 1/5th Leicesters
139th Brigade
1/5th Sherwood Foresters
1/6th Sherwood Foresters
1/7th Sherwood Foresters
1/8th Sherwood Foresters
Pioneers: 1/Monmouths

47th (1/2nd London) Division (T.F.)

Major General Sir C. St L. Barter
(relieved) then Major General G.F.
Gorringe

140th Brigade
1/6th Londons (City of London)
1/7th Londons (City of London)
1/8th Londons (Post Office Rifles)
1/15th Londons (Civil Service Rifles)
141st Brigade
1/17th Londons (Poplar and Stepney Rifles)
1/18th Londons (London Irish Rifles)
1/19th Londons (St Pancras)
1/20th Londons (Blackheath and
Woolwich)
142nd Brigade
1/21st Londons (1st Surrey Rifles)
1/22nd Londons (The Queen's)
1/23rd Londons
1/24th Londons (The Queen's)
Pioneers: 1/4th Royal Welch Fusiliers

48th Division (South Midland) Division (T.F.)

Major General R. Fanshawe

143rd Brigade
1/5th Royal Warwicks
1/16th Royal Warwicks
1/7th Royal Warwicks
1/8th Royal Warwicks
144th Brigade
1/4th Glosters
1/6th Glosters
1/7th Worcestershires
1/8th Worcestershires
145th Brigade
1/5th Glosters
1/4th Oxfordshire and Buckinghamshire
Light Infantry
1/1st Buckinghamshires
1/4th Royal Berkshires
Pioneers: 1/5th Sussex

49th (West Riding) Division (T.F.)

Major General E.M. Perceval

146th Brigade
1/5th West Yorkshires, 1/6th West Yorkshires
1/7th West Yorkshires, 1/8th West Yorkshires

147th Brigade
1/4th Duke of Wellington's
1/5th Duke of Wellington's
1/6th Duke of Wellington's
1/7th Duke of Wellington's

148th Brigade
1/4th King's Own Yorkshire Light Infantry
1/5th King's Own Yorkshire Light Infantry
1/4th York and Lancaster
1/5th York and Lancaster

Pioneers: 3/Monmouth (Replaced by
  19/Lancashire Fusiliers 6 August)

50th (Northumbrian) Division (T.F.)

Major General P.S. Wilkinson

149th Brigade
1/4th Northumberland Fusiliers
1/5th Northumberland Fusiliers
1/6th Northumberland Fusiliers
1/7th Northumberland Fusiliers

150th Brigade
1/4th East Yorkshires, 1/4th Green Howards
1/5th Green Howards
1/5th Durham Light Infantry

151st Brigade
1/5th Borders
1/6th Durham Light Infantry
1/8th Durham Light Infantry
1/9th Durham Light Infantry

Pioneers: 1/7th Durham Light Infantry

51st (Highland) Division (T.F.)

Major General G.M. Harper

152nd Brigade
1/5th Seaforths, 1/6th Seaforths
1/6th Gordons
1/8th Argyll and Sutherlands

153rd Brigade
1/6th Black Watch, 1/7th Black Watch
1/5th Gordons
1/7th Gordons

154th Brigade
1/9th Royal Scots, 1/4th Seaforths
1/4th Gordons
1/7th Argyll and Sutherlands

Pioneers: 1/8th Royal Scots

55th (West Lancashire) Division (T.F.)

Major General H.S. Jeudwine

164th Brigade
1/4th King's Own, 1/8th King's
2/5th Lancashire Fusiliers
1/4th Loyal North Lancashires

165th Brigade
1/5th King's, 1/6th King's
1/7th King's, 1/9th King's

166th Brigade
1/5th King's Own, 1/10th King's
1/5th South Lancashires
1/5th Loyal North Lancashires

Pioneers: 1/4th South Lancashires

56th (1/1st London) Division (T.F.)

Major General C.P.A. Hull

167th Brigade
1/1st Londons (Royal Fusiliers)
1/3rd Londons (Royal Fusiliers)
1/7th Middlesex, 1/8th Middlesex

168th Brigade
1/4th Londons (Royal Fusiliers)
1/12th Londons Rangers
1/13th Londons (Kensington)
1/14th Londons (London Scottish)

169th Brigade
1/2nd Londons (Royal Fusiliers)
1/5th Londons (London Rifle Brigade)
1/9th Londons (Queen Victoria's Rifles)
1/16th London (Queen's Westminster
Rifles)

Pioneers: 1/5th Cheshires

63rd (Royal Navy) Division

Major General Sir A. Paris (wounded)
  then Major General C.D. Shute

188th Brigade
Anson Battalion, Howe Battalion
1/Royal Marine Battalion
2/Royal Marine Battalion

189th Brigade
Hood Batttalion, Nelson Battalion
Hawke Battalion, Drake Battalion

190th Brigade
1/Honourable Artillery Company
7/Royal Fusiliers, 4/Bedfords
10/Royal Dublin Fusiliers

Pioneers: 14/Worcestershires

1st Australian Division

Major General H.B. Walker

1st (New South Wales) Brigade
1st Battalion, 2nd Battalion
3rd Battalion, 4th Battalion
2nd (Victoria) Brigade
5th Battalion, 6th Battalion
7th Battalion, 8th Battalion
3rd Brigade
9th (Queensland) Battalion
10th (S Australia) Battalion
11th (W Australia) Battalion
12th (S and W Australia, Tas.) Battalion
Pioneers: 1st Australian Pioneer Battalion

2nd Australian Division

Major General J.G. Legge

5th (New South Wales) Brigade
17th Battalion, 18th Battalion
19th Battalion, 20th Battalion
6th (Victoria) Brigade
21st Battalion, 22nd Battalion
23rd Battalion, 24th Battalion
7th Brigade
25th (Queensland) Battalion
26th (Q'land, Tas.) Battalion
27th (S Australia) Battalion
28th (W Australia) Battalion
Pioneers: 2nd Australian Pioneer Battalion

4th Australian Division

Major General Sir H. Cox

4th Brigade
13th (New South Wales) Battalion
14th (Victoria) Battalion
15th (Q'land, Tas.) Battalion
16th (S and W Australia) Battalion
12th Brigade
45th (New South Wales) Battalion
46th (Victoria) Battalion
47th (Q'land, Tas.) Battalion
48th (S and W Australia) Battalion
13th Brigade
49th (Queensland) Battalion
50th (S Australia) Battalion
51st (W Australia) Battalion
52nd (S and W Australia, Tas.) Battalion
Pioneers: 4th Australian Pioneer Battalion

5th Australian Division

Major General the Honourable J.W. McCay

8th Brigade
29th (Victoria) Battalion
30th (New South Wales) Battalion
31st (Q'land, Vic.) Battalion
32nd (S and W Australia) Battalion
14th (New South Wales) Brigade
53rd Battalion, 54th Battalion
55th Battalion, 56th Battalion
15th (Victoria) Brigade
57th Battalion, 58th Battalion
59th Battalion, 60th Battalion
Pioneers: 5th Australian Pioneer Battalion

1st Canadian Division

Major General A.W. Currie

1st Brigade
1st (Ontario) Battalion
2nd (East Ontario) Battalion
3rd Battalion (Toronto Regiment)
4th Battalion
2nd Brigade
5th (Western Cavalry) Battalion
7th Battalion (1st British Columbia)
8th Battalion (90th Rifles)
10th Battalion
3rd Brigade
13th Battalion (Royal Highlanders)
14th Battalion (R. Montreal Reg.)
15th Battalion (48th Highlanders)
16th Battalion (Canadian Scottish)
Pioneers: 1st Canadian Pioneer Battalion

2nd Canadian Division

Major General R.E.W. Turner

4th Brigade
18th (W Ontario) Battalion
19th (Central Ontario) Battalion
20th (Central Ontario) Battalion
21st (Eastern Ontario) Battalion
5th Brigade
22nd (Canadien Français) Battalion
24th Battalion (Victoria Rifles)
25th Battalion (Nova Scotia Rifles)
26th (New Brunswick) Battalion
6th Brigade
27th (City of Winnipeg) Battalion
28th (North-West) Battalion

29th (Vancouver) Battalion
31st (Alberta) Battalion
Pioneers: 2nd Canadian Pioneer Battalion

3rd Canadian Division

Major General L.J. Lipsett

7th Brigade
Princess Patricia's Canadian Light Infantry
Royal Canadian Regiment
42nd Battalion (Royal Highlanders)
49th (Edmonton) Battalion

8th Brigade
1st Canadian Mounted Rifles
2nd Canadian Mounted Rifles
4th Canadian Mounted Rifles
5th Canadian Mounted Rifles

9th Brigade
43rd Battalion (Cameron Highlanders)
52nd (New Ontario) Battalion
58th Battalion
60th Battalion (Victoria Rifles)
Pioneers: 3rd Canadian Pioneer Battalion

4th Canadian Division

Major General D. Watson

10th Brigade
44th Battalion
46th (S. Saskatchewan) Battalion

47th (British Columbia) Battalion
50th (Calgary) Battalion

11th Brigade
54th (Kootenay) Battalion
75th (Mississauga) Battalion
87th Battalion (Canadian Grenadier
  Guards)
102nd Battalion

12th Brigade
38th (Ottawa) Battalion
72nd Battalion (Seaforth Highlanders)
73rd Battalion (Royal Highlanders)
78th Battalion (Winnipeg Grenadiers)
Pioneers: 67th Canadian Pioneer Battalion

New Zealand Division

Major General Sir A.H. Russell

1st New Zealand Brigade
1/Auckland, 1/Canterbury,
1/Otago, 1/Wellington

2nd New Zealand Brigade
2/Auckland, 2/Canterbury,
2/Otago, 2/Wellington

3rd New Zealand Rifle Brigade
1/New Zealand Rifle Brigade
2/New Zealand Rifle Brigade
3/New Zealand Rifle Brigade
4/New Zealand Rifle Brigade
Pioneers: New Zealand Pioneer Battalion

Source for orders of battle: *Military Operations, France and Belgium 1916*, Vol. II,
Appendices

1   With 23rd Division until 15th July, in exchange for 70th Brigade
2   Exchanged with 110th Brigade of 37th Division, 7 July
3   With 8th Division until 15 July in exchange for 24th Brigade
4   Replaced by 5th/6th Royal Scots, 29 July
5   Replaced by 12/L.N. Lancs., 19 October
6   Attached to 37th Division 7 July–21 August. Replaced by 111th Brigade
7   Attached to 37th Division 7 July–21 August. Replaced by 112th Brigade
8   Attached to 37th Division 7 July–21 August. Replaced by 9/North Staffordshire
9   Exchanged with 63rd Brigade, 21st Division, 7 July
10 Attached 7 July–21 August to 34th Division
11 Attached 7 July–21 August to 34th Division
12 Attached 7 July–21 August to 34th Division

APPENDIX B

GERMAN ORDER OF BATTLE

3rd Guard Division
Guards Fusiliers, Lehr Regiment
Grenadier Regiment No. 9
4th Guard Division
5th Guards Foot, 5th Guards Grenadiers
Reserve Regiment No. 93
5th Division
Grenadier Regiments Nos. 8 and 12
Regiment No. 52
6th Division
Regiments Nos. 20, 24 and 64
7th Division
Regiments Nos. 26, 27[1] and 165
8th Division
Regiments Nos. 72, 93 and 153
12th Division
Regiments Nos. 23, 62 and 63
16th Division
Regiments Nos. 28, 29, 68 and 69
24th Division
Regiments Nos. 133, 139 and 179
26th Division
Grenadier Regiment No. 119
Regiments Nos. 121 and 125

27th Division
Regiment No. 120
Grenadier Regiment No. 123
Regiments Nos. 124 and 127
38th Division
Regiments Nos. 94, 95 and 96
40th Division
Regiments Nos. 104, 134 and 181
52nd Division
Regiments Nos. 66, 161 and 170
56th Division
Fusilier Regiment No. 35
Regiments Nos. 88 and 118
58th Division
Regiments Nos. 106 and 107
Reserve Regiment No. 120
111th Division
Fusilier Regiment No. 73
Regiments Nos. 76 and 164
117th Division
Regiment No. 157
Reserve Regiments Nos. 11 and 22
183rd Division
Regiments Nos. 183 and 184
Reserve Regiment No. 122

185th Division[2]
Regiments Nos. 185, 186 and 190
208th Division
Regiments Nos. 25 and 185
Reserve Regiment No. 65
222nd Division
Regiments Nos. 193 and 397
Reserve Regiment No. 81
223rd Division
Regiments Nos. 144 and 173
Ersatz Regiment No. 29
1st Guard Reserve Division
Guards Reserve Regiments Nos. 1 and 2
Reserve Regiment No. 64
2nd Guard Reserve Division
Reserve Regiments Nos. 15, 55, 77 and 91
7th Reserve Division
Reserve Regiments Nos. 36, 66 and 72
12th Reserve Division
Reserve Regiments Nos. 23, 38 and 51
17th Reserve Division
Regiments Nos. 162 and 163
Reserve Regiments Nos. 75[3] and 76
18th Reserve Division
Reserve Regiments Nos. 31, 84 and 86
19th Reserve Division
Reserve Regiments Nos. 73, 78, 79 and 92
23rd Reserve Division
Reserve Grenadier Regiment No. 101
Reserve Regiments Nos. 101 and 102
Regiment No. 392
24th Reserve Division
Reserve Regiments Nos. 101, 107 and 133
26th Reserve Division
Reserve Regiments Nos. 99, 119, 121
Regiment No. 180
28th Reserve Division
Reserve Regiments Nos. 109, 110 and 111

45th Reserve Division
Reserve Regiments Nos. 210, 211 and 212
50th Reserve Division
Reserve Regiments Nos. 229, 230 and 231
51st Reserve Division
Reserve Regiments Nos. 233, 234, 235 and 236
52nd Reserve Division
Reserve Regiments Nos. 238, 239 and 240
4th Ersatz Division
Regiments Nos. 359, 360, 361 and 362
5th Ersatz Division
Landwehr Regiments Nos. 73 and 74
Reserve Ersatz Regiment No. 3
2nd Bavarian Division
Bavarian Regiments Nos. 12, 15 and 20
3rd Bavarian Division
Bavarian Regiments Nos. 17, 18 and 23
4th Bavarian Division
Bavarian Regiments Nos. 5 and 9
Bavarian Reserve Regiment No. 5
5th Bavarian Division
Bavarian Regiments Nos. 7, 14, 19 and 21
6th Bavarian Division
Bavarian Regiments Nos. 6, 10, 11 and 13
10th Bavarian Division
Bavarian Regiment No. 16
Bavarian Reserve Regiments Nos. 6 and 8
6th Bavarian Reserve Division
Bavarian Reserve Regiments Nos. 16, 17, 20 and 21
Bavarian Ersatz Division
Bavarian Reserve Regiments Nos. 14 and 15
Ersatz Regiment No. 28
89th Reserve Brigade
Reserve Regiments Nos. 209 and 213
Marine Brigade
Marine Regiments Nos. 1, 2 and 3

---

1   Replaced by Regiment No. 393 for second tour
2   Reorganised for second tour, composition being Regiments Nos. 65, 161 and Reserve Regiment No. 28
3   left division before second tour

FURTHER READING

The chronological and analytical framework of this book was established by using the volumes of the British official history: J.E. Edmonds, *Military Operations, France and Belgium, 1916* (London, 1932), vol. i and W. Miles, *Military Operations, France and Belgium, 1916* (London, 1938), vol ii, supplemented by Chris McCarthy, *The Somme: The Day-by-Day Account* (London, 1993); Martin Middlebrook, *The First Day on the Somme* (London, 1971) and Robin Prior and Trevor Wilson, *Command on the Western Front* (Oxford, 1992).

General Works

A.H. Farrah-Hockley, *The Somme* (London, 1964), although rather dated, still repays reading. Malcolm Brown, *The Imperial War Museum Book of the Somme* (London, 1996) examines the battle through the eyes of the ordinary soldier. Gerald Gliddon, *When the Barrage Lifts* (London, 1990) adopts an unusual approach, using various locations on the Somme as a hook on which to hang anecdotes. Michael Chappell, *The Somme 1916: Crucible of a British Army* (London, 1995) and Martin Marix Evans, *The Battles of the Somme* (London, 1996) are two brief and well-illustrated accounts, either of which would serve as a useful introduction to the battle. Peter Simkins's book in the Osprey 'Essential History' series, *The First World War (1) The Western Front 1914–1916* contains a stimulating account of the Somme by a leading historian. Also useful are the accounts of the Somme by Richard Holmes in *Western Front* (London, 1999) and Andy Simpson, *The Evolution of Victory* (London, 1995).

Gary Sheffield, *Forgotten Victory: The First World War – Myths and Realities* (Headline, 2001) gives a revisionist view of the war, concentrating on the Anglo-American experience, while Ian Beckett, *The Great War 1914–1918* (Longman, 2001) is an erudite but accessible book that gives global coverage of the war. Trevor Wilson, *The Myriad Faces of War* (Cambridge, 1988) gives comprehensive coverage of every aspect of Britain's war. For a good study of all aspects of Germany's war, see Holger H. Herwig, *The First World War: Germany and Austria-Hungary 1914–1918* (London, 1997). Inter-war volumes of the *Army Quarterly* and *Journal of the Royal United Services Institution* are a treasure-trove of articles, including material from the French and German perspectives.

Specialist Studies

Peter Simkins, *Kitchener's Army* (Manchester, 1988) is the definitive account of the raising of the New Armies. For strategy, see David French, *British Strategy and War Aims 1914–1916* (London, 1986) and William Philpott, *Anglo-French Relations and Strategy on the Western Front, 1914–18* (London, 1996). Brock Millman, *Pessimism and British War Policy 1916–1918* (London, 2001) gives a stimulating and original account of British strategy in the aftermath of the Somme.

John Terraine's biography *Douglas Haig: The Educated Soldier* (London, 1963) is unashamedly biased in favour of its subject but has yet to be superseded; it should however be read in conjunction with Brian Bond and Nigel Cave (eds.), *Haig, A Reappraisal 70 Years On* (London, 1999) which contains much up-to-date scholarly thinking about Haig. Tim Travers's important book *The Killing Ground* (London, 1987) is critical of Haig's conduct of the battle. The BEF's tactics on the Somme are well covered by Paddy Griffith, *Battle Tactics of the Western Front* (London, 1994) and Bill Rawling, *Surviving Trench Warfare: Technology and the Canadian Corps 1914–1918* (Toronto, 1992). For the air war, see Peter Hart, *Somme Success: The Royal Flying Corps and the Battle of the Somme, 1916* (Barnsley, 2001), an effective blend of narrative, first-hand accounts and analysis.

For morale and combat motivation, see G.D. Sheffield, *Leadership in the Trenches: Officer–Man Relations, Morale and Discipline in the British Army in the Era of the Great War* (London, 2000) and John Keegan, *The Face of Battle* (Harmondsworth, 1976); the latter includes a detailed examination of 1 July 1916. There are hundreds, if not thousands, of published memoirs, letters and diaries by men who fought on the Somme. One outstanding book which has recently been republished is Rowland Fielding, *War Letters to a Wife* (Staplehurst, 2001). Fielding served as an officer with the Coldstream Guards and then the Connaught Rangers on the Somme. To this must be added an autobiographical novel by a man who served in the ranks of 3rd Division on the Somme, Frederic Manning, *The Middle Parts of Fortune* (London, 1977) which is a strong contender for the title of the finest piece of fiction to emerge from the Great War.

NOTES

Chapter 1: The Road to the Somme

1   General Balck, *Development of Tactics – World War* (Fort Leavenworth, KS, 1922), p.72.
2   W[ar] D[iary] 2nd Div., appx 905, Dec. 1915, WO 95/1288, P[ublic] R[ecord] O[ffice].
3   J.E. Edmonds, *Military Operations, France and Belgium, 1916* (London, 1932), vol.i, appx 1, p.40. This is the British Official History, henceforth abbreviated to 'BOH'; the second volume was published in 1938 and authored by W. Miles. The appendices to both volumes were published in separate books.
4   W. Diest, 'Strategy and Unlimited Warfare in Germany' in R. Chickering and S. Forster, *Great War, Total War: Combat and Mobilization on the Western Front, 1914–1918* (Cambridge, 2000), pp.271–4.
5   H.H. Herwig, *The First World War: Germany and Austria–Hungary 1914–1918* (London, 1997), pp.179–82, 196–7; R.T. Foley, 'Attrition: Its Theory and Application in German Strategy, 1880–1916', Ph.D. thesis, University of London, 1999.
6   R. Blake (ed.), *The Private Papers of Douglas Haig* (29 Mar 1916) (London, 1951), p.137.
7   This following section has been influenced by W.J. Philpott, 'Why the British were Really on the Somme: A Reply to Elizabeth Greenhalgh', forthcoming in *War in History*. I am indebted to Dr Philpott for providing me with a copy of this paper.
8   J. Joffre, *The Memoirs of Marshal Joffre* (London, 1932), vol. ii, p.407.
9   WO 158/19, PRO, reproduced in *Journal of Military History*, 65 (Oct. 2001) pp.1061–5.
10 W.J. Philpott, *Anglo-French Relations and Strategy on the Western Front, 1914–18* (London, 1996), p.128.
11 J. Charteris, *At G.H.Q.* (London, 1931), p.151.
12 Letter, n[ot] d[ated], in CAB 45/134, PRO.
13 G.C. Wynne, *If Germany Attacks* (London, 1940), p.103.
14 WD Reserve Army, appx 1 to July 1916, WO 95/518, PRO.
15 Quoted in Sir F. Maurice, *The Life of Lord Rawlinson of Trent* (London, 1928), p.130.
16 *A[rmy] Q[uarterly]*, Oct. 1934, p.31.
17 German Official History, quoted in *Army Quarterly* (Jul. 1937) pp.223–36.
18 Foley, 'Attrition',170, 229–30.
19 'Synopsis of lectures…' WO 107/8, PRO.
20 Trenchard Papers, MFC 76/1/4, RAF Museum.

21 D. Jordan, 'The Battle for the Skies: Sir Hugh Trenchard as Commander of the Royal Flying Corps' in M. Hughes and M. Seligmann (eds.), *Leadership in Conflict 1914–1918* (London, 2000), pp.77–8.

22 H.L. Pritchard (ed.), *History of the Corps of Royal Engineers* (Chatham, 1952), vol v, pp. 253–76.

23 Second Lieutenant E.W. Harris, diary, 30 June 1916, Liddle Collection, University of Leeds.

24 Appx C, July 1916, WO 95/523.

25 I.M. Brown, *British Logistics on the Western Front 1914–1919* (Westport, CT, 1998) p.125.

26 E.G.D. Living, *Attack on the Somme* (Stevenage, 1986) p.20.

27 R. Prior and T. Wilson, *Command on the Western Front* (Oxford, 1992) pp.166–70.

28 M. Middlebrook, *The First Day on the Somme* (London, 1971), p.121. The last sentence is a quote from a soldier of 18th Division.

Chapter 2: The First Day on the Somme

1   J. Harris, *Covenant with Death* (London, 1961), p.382. This book is based on the experience of the Sheffield City Battalion.

2   G. Malins, *How I Filmed the War*, new edition (London, 1993) pp. 162–3.

3   BOH, I, 435.

4   Middlebrook, *First Day*, 188–9.

5   J.H. Boraston and C.E.O. Bax, *The Eighth Division 1914–1918* (London, new edition,1999) pp.68–76.

6   Boraston and Bax, *Eighth Division*, 74–5.

7   Middlebrook, *First Day*, 98–9, 261.

8   J. Shakespeare, *The 34th Division* (London, new edition, n.d.) p.25.

9   G.H.F. Nichols, *The 18th Division in the Great War* (London, 1922), p.2.

10 BOH 1916, i, 326. Another version has the two men simply shaking hands on the objective.

11 Marchal Fayolle (H. Contamine, ed.), *Cahiers Secrets de la Grande Guerre* (Paris, 1964), p.165.

12 BOH 1916, i, 485.

13 R. Prior and T. Wilson, *Command on the Western Front* (Oxford, 1992), pp.166–70.

14 Jonathon Bailey, *The First World War and the Birth of the Modern Style of Warfare* (Camberley, SCSI Occasional Paper No. 22, 1996).

15 A. Simpson, *The Evolution of Victory* (London, 1995), p.59.

16 P. Griffith, *Battle Tactics of the Western Front* (New Haven, CT, 1994), pp.56–64.

17 P. Simkins, 'Everyman at War' in B. Bond (ed.), *The First World War and British Military History* (Oxford, 1991), pp.304–5.

Chapter 3: The Second Phase: July 1916

1   Joffre, *Memoirs*, ii, 477.

2   Prior and Wilson, *Command on the Western Front*, 187–9.

3   All quotations in this paragraph are taken from T.R. Moreman, 'The Dawn Assault – Friday 14th July 1916', *Journal of the Society of Army Historical Research* (Autumn 1993), pp.181–2.

4   C.T. Atkinson, *The Seventh Division 1914–1918* (London, 1927), p.282.

5   C. Bonham-Carter, letter to family, 14 July 1916, BCHT 2/1, Charles Bonham-Carter Papers, C[hurchill] C[ollege] C[ambridge].

6   Prior and Wilson, *Command on the Western Front*, 191–2.

7   S. Badsey, 'Cavalry and the Development of Breakthrough Doctrine' in P. Griffith
    (ed.), *British Fighting Methods in the Great War* (London, 1996), pp.153–7.
8   C. Falls, *Marshal Foch* (London, 1939), pp.105–6.
9   Fayolle, *Cahiers Secrets*, 165.
10 Balck, *Development of Tactics*, 75.
11 Foley, 'Attrition', 234.
12 Prior and Wilson, *Command on the Western Front*, 203–5.
13 H.O. Montieth memoirs, p.51, 3 DRL 7340, A[ustralian W[ar] M[emorial].

Chapter 4: Attrition and Attempted Breakthrough

1   29 July 1916, WO 95/1368, PRO.
2   SS 487, 'Order of the 6th Bavarian Division Regarding Machine Guns, 3 Sept. 1916',
    E 434, JSCSC Library.
3   J.O. Coop, *The Story of the 55th (West Lancashire) Division* (Liverpool, 1919),
    pp.31–2.
4   OAD 91, 2 August 1916, in BOH 1916, ii, appx 13.
5   Introduction to C. McCarthy, *The Somme: The Day-by-Day Account* (London,
    1993), p.10.
6   R. Berkeley, *The History of the Rifle Brigade in the War of 1914–1918* (London,
    1927), vol.1 pp.175–6.
7   C.E. Crutchley, *Machine Gunner 1914–1918* (London, 1975), pp.52–3.
8   M. Kincaid-Smith, *The 25th Division in France and Flanders* (London, n.d.), p.18.
9   E. Jünger, *The Storm of Steel* (New York, new edition, 1985), pp.102, 107–10.
10 T. Denman, *Ireland's Unknown Soldiers* (Co. Dublin, 1992), pp.97–8, 100.
11 In A.F. Wedd (ed.), *German Students' War Letters* (London, 1929), pp.322–3.
12 BOH 1916, ii, 560.
13 E. von Falkenhayn, *General Headquarters 1914–1916 and its Critical Decisions*
    (London, 1919) p.292.
14 G. Feldman, quoted in R. Chickering, *Imperial Germany and the Great War,
    1914–1918* (Cambridge, 1998) p.82.
15 Balck, *Development of Tactics*, 80.
16 J.P. Harris, *Men, Ideas and Tanks* (Manchester, 1995), p.62.
17 Prior and Wilson, *Command on the Western Front*, 239.
18 Prior and Wilson, *Command on the Western Front*, 233.
19 C. Headlam, *History of the Guards Division in the Great War 1915–1918* (London,
    1924), vol i, p.161.
20 H.A. Jones, *The War in the Air* (London, 1928), vol. ii, pp.274–5.
21 T. Pidgeon, *The Tanks at Flers* (Cobham, 1995), p.168.
22 H. Stewart, *The New Zealand Division 1916–1919* (Auckland, 1921), pp.75–6.
23 T. Norman, *The Hell They Called High Wood* (London, 1989), p.233.
24 Pidgeon, *Tanks at Flers*, 133.
25 Wedd, *German Students' War Letters*, 372–3.
26 P. Simkins in McCarthy, *The Somme*, 10.
27 W.E. Drury, *Camp Follower* (Dublin, 1968), pp.103, 105.

Chapter 5: Morval to the Ancre

1   P. Hart, *Somme Success: The Royal Flying Corps and the Battle of the Somme, 1916*
    (Barnsley, 2001), pp.174–9.
2   G.H. Lewis, *Wings over the Somme 1916–1918* (London, 1976), pp.93–4.
3   S.F. Wise, *Canadian Airmen and the First World War* (Toronto, 1980), pp.386, 390.
4   Prior and Wilson, *Command on the Western Front*, 247.

5   F. Ponsonby, *The Grenadier Guards in the Great War of 1914 to 1918* (London, 1920), vol. ii, p.138.
6   Coop, *Story of the 55th Division*, 42.
7   F.I. Maxse, *The 18th Division in the Battle of the Ancre* 'printed report, Dec. 1918', pp.3–4.
8   Anon, *The 54th Infantry Brigade 1914–1918* (Aldershot, n.d.) p.51.
9   *AQ* (July 1937), p.314.
10 Tim Cook, 'The Blood Test of Battle: The Learning Curve of the Four Canadian Infantry Divisions, 1914–1916'. I am extremely grateful to Mr Cook for making this unpublished paper available to me.
11 Jones, *War in the Air*, 284.
12 Jones, *War in the Air*, 298.
13 V.E. Inglefield, *The History of the Twentieth (Light) Division* (London, 1921), p.102.
14 Jones, *War in the Air*, 303.
15 Anon, *Sixteenth, Seventeenth, Eighteenth, Nineteenth Battalions The Manchester Regiment: A Record 1914–1918* (Manchester, 1922), pp.303–4.
16 C.E.W. Bean, *Anzac to Amiens* (Canberra, new edition, 1968), p.267.
17 Blake, *Private Papers of Douglas Haig* (Haig diary, 23 Oct. 1916), 173.
18 Philpott, *Anglo-French Relations*, 127; BOH 1916, ii, 458–9, 474.
19 C.H. Dudley Ward, *Regimental Records of the Royal Welch Fusiliers* (London, 1928), vol. iii, p.253.
20 C.E. Carrington, *Soldier from the Wars Returning* (London, 1965), p.129.
21 Quoted in Paul Reed, *Battleground Europe: Walking the Somme* (London, 1997), p.199.
22 See S.A. Hart, *Montgomery and 'Colossal Cracks': the 21st Army Group in Northwest Europe, 1944–45* (Westport, CT, 2000).
23 Chris Page, 'The Royal Naval Division 1914–19' in Peter Hore (ed.), *Seapower Ashore: 200 Years of Royal Navy Operations on Land* (London, 2001), pp.222–3.
24 E. Ludendorff, *My War Memories 1914–1918* (London, n.d.), vol. i, p.290.

Chapter 6: The Aftermath

1   Herwig, *First World War*, 204; R. Holmes, *Western Front* (London, 1999), p.139.
2   M. & M. Middlebrook, *The Somme Battlefields* (London, 1991), pp.353–4.
3   M. MacDonagh, *In London During the Great War* (London, 1935), pp.146–7.
4   K. Jeffrey, *Ireland and the Great War* (Cambridge, 2000), p.59.
5   J. Jolliffe (ed.), *Raymond Asquith: Life and Letters* (London, 1987), p.294.
6   H. Brennert, *Bei unferen Helden an der Somme* (York, new edition, 1998).
7   H. Sulzbach, *With the German Guns* (London, 1981), p.96.
8   Ludendorff, *War Memories*, 304.
9   *AQ* (July 1937), p.314.
10 J. Terraine, *The Smoke and the Fire* (London, 1980), pp.124–5.
11 *AQ* (July 1937), pp.13–14.
12 H.A. Gwynne to H.H. Asquith, 9 November 1916, copy in Rawlinson Papers, RWLN 1/8, CCC.
13 Ludendorff, *War Memories*, 307.
14 Figures are from Middlebrook, *Somme Battlefields*, 111, 166, 351.
15 C. Falls, *The First World War* (London, 1960), p.178.

INDEX